Dear Gladys

Marie-Louise von Franz, Honorary Patron

**Studies in Jungian Psychology
by Jungian Analysts**

Daryl Sharp, General Editor

Dear Gladys

The Survival Papers
Book 2

Daryl Sharp

To Norman and all he stands for.

Canadian Cataloguing in Publication Data

Sharp, Daryl, 1936-
   Dear Gladys: the survival papers, book 2

(Studies in Jungian psychology by Jungian analysts; 37)

Includes bibliographical references and index.

ISBN 0-919123-36-8

1. Middle age—Psychological aspects—Case Studies.
2. Life change events—Case studies. 3. Jung, C.G.
(Carl Gustav), 1875-1961. 4. Psychoanalysis.
5. Sharp, Daryl, 1936- . I. Title. II. Title: The
survival papers, book 2. III. Series.

BF724.6.S47 1989   155.6   C88-095233-4

Copyright © 1989 by Daryl Sharp.
All rights reserved.

INNER CITY BOOKS
Box 1271, Station Q, Toronto, Canada M4T 2P4
Telephone (416) 927-0355

Honorary Patron: Marie-Louise von Franz.
Publisher and General Editor: Daryl Sharp.
Senior Editor: Victoria Cowan.
Editorial Board: Fraser Boa, Daryl Sharp, Marion Woodman.
Production: David Sharp.

INNER CITY BOOKS was founded in 1980 to promote the
understanding and practical application of the work of C.G. Jung.

Cover: Four views of *Self-portrait of Pissarro,* 1983, spectral
hologram by Canadian artist Jerry Pethick (Publisher's Collection).
Photography by Robin Roddey.

Index by Daryl Sharp.

Printed and bound in Canada by Webcom Limited

CONTENTS

Preface 9

Introduction 11

1 Work on What Has Been Spoiled 15

2 Norman Takes a Flyer 31

3 Dear Gladys 42

4 Enter the Dragon 58

5 Look Homeward, Devil 72

6 Mirror, Mirror, Tell Me True 85

7 The Worm Turns 88

8 Invitation to a Beheading 105

9 Rachel Pulls a Fast One 115

10 The Lazarus Heart 117

11 The Beginning of the End 133

Epilogue 137

Index 139

See final pages for descriptions of other Inner City Books

The true history of the spirit is not preserved in learned volumes but in the living psychic organism of every individual.
—C.G. Jung, "Psychology and Religion."

Preface

The story so far:
Norman was a successful businessman who at the age of thirty fell in love with Nancy. Nancy became pregnant. Norman and Nancy got married. They had two children. Norman loved his family but he was not happy. Norman fell apart when he was thirty-six years old. He went into Jungian analysis on his knees. After a year he left his family. After two years he left his analyst.

The underlying psychology of a breakdown and Norman's first year in analysis are detailed in *The Survival Papers: Anatomy of a Midlife Crisis*. Norman's second year in analysis, during which he found his feet and lived to writhe again, was in that book passed over rather quickly.

Readers have clamored to have this interval fleshed out.

This book is a response to that clamor.

Introduction

"Did you hear me?" said Rachel.

"I wasn't listening," I pretended.

I was rummaging in a box of old letters. Rachel is my anima. We have our problems, but on the whole I wouldn't know what to do without her. She was perched on my desk, tapping her knee with a dog-eared copy of *The Survival Papers*.

"I don't understand," Rachel repeated, "how you can go on writing about Norman as if he were a real person, when you've already said you made him up."

"I exaggerated to make a point."

"So is he you?"

I considered.

"There's much of me in Norman," I conceded. "Our psychology is similar and we share certain behavior patterns. But that doesn't distinguish us from the bulk of mankind. There isn't *one* Norman, there are *millions* of Normans. What I wrote about could happen to anyone. And in some cases, with me, it did."

I thought of something else.

"I shouldn't have said Norman's story was fiction, I should have called it a conceit. Do you know what that is?"

"Having too high an opinion of yourself?" she asked slyly.

I looked at her.

"I was thinking of another meaning of the word. Here," I pulled out the American Heritage Dictionary and read: " 'Conceit—an elaborate or exaggerated metaphor.' The description of Norman's psychology is sound. I simply created a metaphorical structure, a context to contain it."

"Do you expect that will get you off the hook?"

I shrugged. "You yourself said you wanted more," I reminded her. "And so do many others. I've had letters from all over the world—accolades, great appreciation."

I took out a folder labeled *Survival Papers: Responses.*

"Listen to this from a fan in Spain: 'It is a wonderful thing you wrote. I congratulate you on your tusk.' "

Rachel smiled. "Task, surely."

"And this one from a group of faithful readers in France: 'We loved Norman and are certainly hopping to hear more of him.' "

"Hoping," said Rachel.

"Nevertheless. Here's a letter from Gordo, my old drinking buddy in Zurich and now an analyst himself: 'This is the best book ever written. You have managed to combine an acute understanding of Jungian theory with the skills of a novelist.' How about that!? The best book *ever written!"*

Rachel frowned. "An overstatement."

"Perhaps," I said, preening.

"You're puffed up like a peacock," observed Rachel. "A few pretty feathers have gone to your head."

"I'm the writer, you're just a muse," I said tartly.

But Rachel was not there.

*

I wandered about forty days then, basking, ignoring the warning dreams. True, I turned down some invitations to speak. But not without a struggle. My friend Arnold, who enjoys the lecture circuit, pressed me to accept.

"Think of the possibilities," he urged. "Fame and glory! Influence! Riches!"

"Dross," I replied, diving into my pool.

I surfaced to hear him say, "You could make a difference!"

I spewed a mouthful of water. "I do not enjoy public speaking. More," I said, finding my true ground, "I do not like to travel."

Arnold jeered. "That's your mother complex. You only feel secure in your own back yard."

I readily agreed. You can't fight the truth. You don't need to be ashamed of it, either.

Arnold and I have had many such exchanges over the years. He sees things in a way I don't, and vice versa. We used to try to understand each other. Now we don't need to. The tension between us manifests as energy.

Between Rachel and Arnold, I had a pretty interesting summer.

Meanwhile, the way to present Norman's second year was taking shape.

*

"You're determined to go ahead?" asked Rachel.

We were in the basement, huddled together like two chickadees. It was the hottest week on record and even the swimming pool was no relief. I had looked into air-conditioning but never got around to it. The basement was the only place cool enough to think. I had moved some cartons of books to make a small working space and hooked up the computer.

"Not so much determined as driven," I said. "I wake up in the middle of the night and can't get back to sleep. I think of new material. I dream about Norman, he's still in my blood. And then there's his wife Nancy. I could say more about her."

I paused. "Not to mention the analyst."

Rachel showed some interest.

"So what do you have in mind? Do you have a plan?"

"It will evolve."

"And if it doesn't?"

I spread my arms. "I'll still have you."

More or less.

Acknowledgment

CW refers throughout to *The Collected Works of C.G. Jung* (Bollingen Series XX), 20 vols., trans. R.F.C. Hull, ed. H. Read, M. Fordham, G. Adler, Wm. McGuire; Princeton: Princeton University Press, 1953-1979.

1
Work on What Has Been Spoiled

The existence of a sense of inner security by no means proves that the product will be stable enough to withstand the disturbing or hostile influence of the environment. . . . More than once everything [one] has built will fall to pieces under the impact of reality.
—C.G. Jung, *Mysterium Coniunctionis.*

Norman plonked himself down on the sofa. Glum, glum. His mood was like a fog between us.

"The world is a turd," he said.

"A turd?" I repeated. Perhaps he had some mythological parallel in mind. I knew that among some Indian tribes in South America human excrement was consecrated to the gods.

"Living alone is the shits," he said, tears in his eyes. "I can't do it, I have to go back."

At this point Norman had been away from his wife and kids for close to two months. He was living in a basement apartment in a run-down part of the city. He had one room, a kitchenette and a bathroom. Every Saturday morning he went to visit his family. He played with the kids, helped with the shopping, did a few odd jobs. On Sunday evening he returned to his cell.

Norman's situation was familiar to me. It was much the same as that of many dislocated fathers. And mothers too. In fact it was a woman who first pointed out to me: "You live alone, you pays your dues. You live with your family, you pays your dues. Either way you pays dues."

"I left because it seemed to me the only way I had a chance," said Norman. "Now I'm not so sure. What if I made the wrong decision? What if it's just an easy way out of my real responsibilities?"

"Not so easy at that," I observed.

"I feel skewered between my anima and my mother complex," he went on. "My anima won't let me live with Nancy, my mother complex won't let me live without her."

Norman had picked up the jargon. I wasn't happy about that, but you can't stop people from reading.

"I made love to Nancy when I was home last weekend," he said. "She did her usual stone act. God, I'm so frustrated!"

The tears welled up. "It's a half-life," he said bitterly. "It's that or nothing at all."

Norman took out a hanky and blew his nose. "On Saturday night I dreamed of Eleanor. Remember her? We had a thing for a few days last year in Des Moines. In the dream she came to visit Nancy and me. I took her down to the basement and explained the situation. The light was very dim. It was like we were in a mine-shaft. As Eleanor left, I called out to her, 'I'm talking to you from the end of a long tunnel!' She was appalled."

I said nothing. Norman was right where he should be. He had a conflict, and only by holding the tension between opposites could he hope to become a free man. In this case, the opposites were living with his family and living alone.

"When I left Sunday night, Nancy put it to me. 'Either come back to stay or don't come back at all,' she said. 'It's too hard on me and the kids can't stand it either.' "

Norman looked out the window. "Nancy says I have no feeling for her. She needs to have men friends, she says. I agree, and then I feel worse! God, I can't stand her suffering! She acts so strong and I know she isn't. Half the time she's crying when I come home. I'm no help to her, I feel like a child. How can I get her to love me?"

He grunted. "You know what? I think she's still seeing Boris."

My heart went out to Norman. I had nothing else to offer, no solutions, no pat answers. He was a victim of his own psychology, no more, no less. His past was a memory, his present was a shambles. After a year of analysis he had taken some major steps, but his future was unknown. The ball was in his park.

"Look at it this way," I said, "it's an opportunity to grow up. If your wife were passionately interested in you, you might still be unconscious. It's a *felix culpa,* like when Eve ate the apple and she and Adam were thrown out of the Garden. According to the Church it was a fortunate crime, the beginning of the history of consciousness. You can't become conscious if you stay in the Garden."

"You mean I'm conscious now?" asked Norman, fishing.

"I was speaking relatively."

He lapsed into silence.

Consciousness is not a one-time thing, it's an on-going struggle. It's like treading water for a lifetime. Sometimes you go under. If you keep your wits about you, you bob back up. If you don't, you sink into the depths.

Norman's fate is largely dependent on unconscious factors. The unconscious is Janus-faced: on the one hand its contents point back to a preconscious, prehistoric world of instinct, while on the other it anticipates the future, even shows the way to it. It is the task of consciousness to endure the open conflict that often exists between the two. It's the old game of hammer and anvil. Between them the individual is forged.

The unconscious is too big to beat, and joining it is to give up the struggle entirely. What is left? You can take a stand toward it. That is called consciousness.

"What do you want?" I asked.

Norman looked bleak. "It's not a question of what I want. More like what I can stand. I have a horror of growing old all alone. I have gray pubic hairs. That's disgusting! I think of being an old man lying in a hospital bed, near the end, and no one comes to say good-by. Nobody loves me! I'm on my own!"

The tears broke through. He fell back and sobbed.

I passed the kleenex.

I was in analysis for about two months before I cried in front of my analyst. Whatever happened outside, in my analytic hours I was determined to be a man. I wanted to impress my analyst, I wanted him to like and respect me. I had an urbane persona to live up to, my image of myself. I would not willingly drop it in front of my analyst. He was the person in whose eyes I most wanted to shine. I never told him how I really felt about anything. I feared he would judge me as weak.

This charade came to an end the day his comments struck a nerve that was so raw my defenses failed. At the time I thought it was quite accidental. Today, having pushed a few buttons myself, I'm not so sure.

I remember it well. It was a bright Thursday morning. That is not normal in Zurich. While the surrounding mountains are bathed in sunshine, the city is invariably overcast and grey. Meteorologically, Zurich invites depression. The weather reports speak of highs and lows. They match one's mood.

My analyst's office was lined with bookshelves. Personal mementos were everywhere. I loved that place. Once a week I sat there for an hour and felt safe.

"It was a good week," I lied.

Should I tell him about my crying in the night? Should I tell him how lonely I was, how I felt about Arnold's interminable parties? Would he be interested to know that I got into bed with two women one night and couldn't get an erection? What would he think if I told him I was afraid of dogs? How would he react to my prowling the bars along the Niederdorf, Zurich's red-light district? Should I tell him about my experiments with dope? About the woman who bit me in a pub?

I forced a smile. "Nothing special."

He was silent.

I read from my journal, my usual routine. I had diligently recorded each day's events—edited to make me look good—followed by the dreams that night and my associations to their bizarre images. I amplified the themes from mythology and religion and reflected at length on their psychological meaning.

No doubt about it, I was really a prize student. I did everything I was supposed to. I could not be faulted on procedure.

"And what else?" asked my analyst, smoothing the top of his head where no hair grew.

"What else what?" I said, looking up.

"What else occurs to you," he said. "What else do you think of ... about this woman in your dream, this unknown female who asks you for a dance?"

"Well, she's my anima, isn't she?"

"I don't speak Greek," said my analyst. "Explain, please."

I leaned back, confident. "The anima is my inner woman," I said. "Everybody knows that. Apparently she wants to get closer to me." I laughed. "I have no objection."

My analyst leaned forward. "That's bullshit," he said.

I cringed. Tears stung my eyes. I opened my mouth to speak and nothing came out. For a few minutes I cried uncontrollably. I also had the hiccoughs.

I wiped my face. "Sorry about that," I said. "I don't know what came over me."

My analyst looked quite stern. His eyes were slightly in shadow from the reading lamp between us. He clasped and unclasped his hands. I felt naked, stripped to the bone. I hung there, expecting to be banished. My eyes took in his books, his antique desk, the lush green plants, an upright piano in one corner, the window looking to the lake. I fastened on his bald spot, waiting. Please God, I thought, do not tell me I'm unworthy.

Then he smiled, openly, a rare breaking of the lips that to me sang of acceptance. He rubbed his hands. "Now we do analysis," he said, "if that's what you want."

That was almost twenty years ago. I still remember that session, and many others, because they were turning points. On that Thursday morning I developed a degree of trust for my analyst that hadn't been there before. I broke down and it was okay.

In this respect Norman had the jump on me. The first time he came he cried the whole hour. He never put on a false front. His feelings were always close to the surface and he didn't try to hide them.

"I went to a party last night," Norman was saying. "There were plenty of girls, but I had no appetite. About midnight I phoned Nancy. She was curt, I'd woken her up. I cried for five minutes. I really wanted to go home.

"Nancy was not happy about that. 'I don't like you like this,' she said, 'I wish you'd work it out.' She finally hung up on me.

"Work it out! Je-suz! What if I can't? What if this is my life?"

I shrugged.

"I'm so ambivalent," said Norman. "Whatever way I turn in my head—to be with her or not—seems right for a few minutes, then it flips. When Nancy is cold, I think I can't go back, I'll die there. But all she has to do is smile or touch me, or look at me like she used to, and those thoughts are out the window. Well yes, I think, I can live with her after all."

I am no stranger to ambivalence. It doesn't always involve women but it invariably goes hand in hand with conflict. One of the lengthiest I ever endured was over a job offer from a publisher I'd been working for while in Zurich. It was a large operation, very classy books. He wanted me to take over as editor-in-chief. I was flattered. The salary was generous. It would be interesting work. But I still had a year to go to finish training.

I talked it over with my analyst. "I don't think I want the job but I can't bring myself to turn it down. What should I do?"

"I don't know," he said.

"Maybe I won't like being an analyst," I fretted. "Don't you ever get bored, listening to people's problems all day?"

"Sometimes it's hard to stay awake." He smiled. "But it keeps me in touch with myself."

My friend Arnold said: "Sure, it's a great opportunity. But think about why we came here in the first place."

At that time Arnold was washing dishes in a posh Zurich café. It was black work, he didn't have a permit. The pay wasn't good but he brought home big bags of cold cuts.

Rachel was elusive in those days, she had nothing meaningful to say.

I went back and forth in my mind for several weeks. The tension was awful. I could not decide.

I finally told the publisher I would accept the job if he added a secretary and I could arrange my schedule to attend classes at the Institute. He agreed.

"You're crazy," said Arnold, "you can't do both."

I panicked. I asked for more money and a travel allowance. The publisher talked to his backers and got the okay.

Now I was terrified.

"What am I going to do?" I said to my analyst. "Every time I make new conditions he accepts them!"

He smiled. "You seem to want him to make your decision. He knows what he wants. Do you?"

After two months of sitting on the fence I rejected the job. The publisher was disappointed. He said only, "I hope you know what you're doing."

At our next session I told my analyst. I thought he'd be proud of me. After all, I'd resisted Mammon.

"Like Christ in the desert, I stood firm."

He said: "An interesting image, but you might have made a better editor than an analyst."

That reconstellated the whole conflict. I had made the right decision, but for the wrong reasons. Now the opposite came back to haunt me. By then the job had gone to someone else, but the conflict didn't die until Arnold threw a party marking my fortieth birthday.

"Look at me!" he said, shuffling along the floor like José Ferrer playing Toulouse Lautrec. "We have nothing to lose but our knees!"

Norman was staring at me. "You're quiet. You don't say much. Where am I in this process?" he said impatiently. "I watch myself. I write. I paint. Why do I still feel so bad? Am I doing the right thing? You don't tell me. I spill my guts and you hardly speak at all. Dammit! I'm not even sure you're listening."

I've heard that before. It used to unnerve me.

"What is it you want to hear?" I said.

"I don't know," replied Norman. "You're the expert."

I shook my head. "No."

"You are!" he insisted. "You've been trained. You know the mysteries, I don't. Tell me what is true. Wipe the scales from my eyes. Show me the light!"

I polished my half-glasses with a tissue, wondering if my Japanese maple would survive the frost. I was not indifferent to Norman's plight, but he had some expectations I couldn't meet. Call it projection, call it transference, he saw me as his savior. It wasn't his fault, that's just the way it is. You invest other people with your own potential. And when they don't live up to it, you get testy.

"I know some theories and I have experienced my own process," I said. "That's all. Your behavior fits some patterns I'm familiar with, but you yourself are unique. I can't plumb your depths, that's up to you. I'm not a mind reader. Be patient. A solution to your life, a way out of the maze, will crystallize in you."

In my head I was hearing my analyst saying something similar. Like Norman I had been frustrated without explicit guidance. I believed my analyst held the key to my life, all those locked doors. It was perverse of him to let me stew.

"Release me," I begged one day.

It was some months after my crying jag. I'd had a particularly difficult week. Money was low, my teeth hurt, my girlfriend thought she was pregnant. Arnold kept me awake at night practicing on his banjo.

"You *know* me," I said, "you can do it."

I clammed up. Already this much, with its implied criticism, took all my courage.

My analyst was not one to make speeches. On that occasion, however, he did not mince words.

"You misunderstand this process," he said. "It's all in your hands. Think of what you have been, what you are and what you could be. Reflect on your material, pay close attention to what happens in your life and talk to me about it. I will listen and from time to time I will respond. If I'm silent it's because I have nothing to say.

"You pay for my time and my integrity. I have no answers, no secret prescription. I work on your process only during our hour together. Outside of analysis I attend to my own life. If you expect more, you will be disappointed. Look on me simply as one of your tools."

You made that up, said Rachel. Be quiet, I said, it's close enough. I smiled at Norman.

"It's not fair!" he said with some heat. "You know things you won't tell me."

I thought a minute. What I knew for sure, I could put in a teacup. And it would still be mostly dregs.

"It's true I could say more than I do. The question is whether it would make any difference. Do you think there is nothing going on between us except what we say to each other? Do you think that's all there is?"

Norman blushed. He had had ample evidence over the past year that the unconscious had a say in everything.

"Healing, if it takes place at all," I said, "has little to do with conscious intentions. You imagine I can heal your wounds. You forget your own inner healer and my wounds." I picked up volume 16 of Jung's *Collected Works*. "Here," I said, "go home and read 'The Psychology of the Transference.'

"Now, let's get back to work. Tell me all your associations to this woman in your dream . . . Eleanor."

*

When Norman left, I thought of the possibility that he was not cut out for analysis, that he might kill himself. It had come up before. In the past, his suicidal thoughts had evaporated as his natural enthusiasm for life took over. I had to trust in that. Suicide is a real option only for those who have no hope. Norman was depressed, but to my mind far from hopeless. He'd tough it out.

Alone that night, I reread Jung's essay. I had forgotten how very good it is. It's all there, the alpha and omega of analysis.

When I first entered analysis it was just another course to me, like being at university. The goal was grades. You did your best and you passed or failed.

This is not what happens in analysis. Here your best is not what you have to offer intellectually, nor is your worst. The goal is individuation, but even that, Jung points out, "is important only as an idea; the essential thing is the *opus*"—the work on yourself—"which leads to the goal; *that* is the goal of a lifetime."[1]

Moreover, you are graded, if at all—and even then not by your analyst—on what is in your heart.

There are a lot of dull hours in analysis when nothing seems to be happening. There is the occasional Eureka!, but sometimes change takes years. The revelations, the insights, come only after prolonged attention to the mundane. This is quite a shock to those who go into analysis seeking the divine.

People have come to me because they wanted to understand their visions. When they realize there is nothing special about having visions, that they're as common as turnips and that their task is to come down to earth, they stop analysis.

People come to me because they *want* to have visions. I send them away. I have a great respect for visions, but I don't know how to create them.

I've seen others who thought analysis would make them gods, invulnerable. They stopped because it doesn't. Some go into analysis just because they think it's a good idea. They don't last long either, there's no edge. And then there are those who stop out of sheer frustration; they can't make the connection between what goes on at night, in their dreams, and everyday life.

Daily life is the raw material of analysis. It's analogous to what the alchemists called the *prima materia*—lead, the base metal they strived to turn into gold. Psychologically this refers to one's moods and dreams, attitudes, feelings, thoughts. And especially the nitty-gritty

---

[1] "The Psychology of the Transference," *The Practice of Psychotherapy*, CW 16, par. 400.

detail, the "he said," "she said" encounters that bring you to a boil but you'd like to forget when you cool down.

All this you write down in a journal. That takes some discipline. If you don't keep a journal, you don't remember.

Of course you can't record everything. You'd get lost in the forest and miss the trees. You note the highlights, particularly emotional reactions—because they signal the presence of complexes—and your conscious attitude toward them. You mull this over and you take it to your analyst.

Time is a big factor in this process. An hour or two a week is never enough, but when it's all you've got you soon get used to it. The real work in any case is what you do between sessions, on your own, or not; and if not, then nothing happens.

I think of Rilke's neighbor, a Russian bureaucrat named Nikolai Kusmitch. Time was precious to Nikolai Kusmitch. He spent his days hoarding it, saving a second here, a minute or two there, sometimes a whole half hour. He imagined that the time he saved could be used to better advantage when he wasn't so busy. Perhaps it could even be tacked on at the end of his life, so he'd live longer.

He sought out what he thought must exist, a state institution for time, a kind of Time Bank you could make deposits in and then draw on. He didn't find one, so he kept the loose change in his head.

Nikolai Kusmitch did what he could to economize, but after a few weeks it struck him that he was spending too much.

"I must retrench," he thought.

He rose earlier. He washed less thoroughly, ate his toast standing up and drank coffee on the run. But on Sundays, when he came to settle his accounts, he always found that nothing remained of his savings. He died as he had lived, a pauper.[2]

Working on yourself is something like that. You can't save it up for Sundays, it's what you do during the week that counts.

---

[2] Rainer Maria Rilke, *The Notebooks of Malte Laurids Brigge*, trans. John Linton (London: The Hogarth Press, 1959), pp. 161ff.

Jung described complexes as islands of consciousness, split off from the ego-mainland. It's a useful metaphor. When you're emotional, caught in a complex, you're cut off from rational ego resources; the complex rules the personality as long as you stay on the island. When the storm dies down you swim ashore and lick your wounds, wondering what got into you.

When you occupy an island most of the time—as Norman does, living on the mother, so to speak—a "monster" is constellated in the surrounding waters, the unconscious. Curiously enough, that creature is one's potential salvation. Jung describes it like this:

> The island is a bit cramped and . . . life on it is pretty meagre and plagued with all sorts of imaginary wants because too much life has been left outside. As a result a terrifying monster is created, or rather is roused out of its slumbers. . . . This seemingly alarming animal stands in a secret compensatory relationship to the island and could supply everything that the island lacks.[3]

One might think the ego has what the island lacks. Well, it doesn't. If it did, the island would not have formed in the first place. Islands are after all only refuges for what is unacceptable to those living on the mainland. The mainland in this context is not so much an ego as a persona, which would like to rid itself of anything unconventional.

I see, said Rachel, like England sending its convicted criminals to Australia. Tsk, tsk, I said, that's just one island dumping its garbage on another.

A human personality is made up of an ego and any number of island complexes. The task in analysis is to establish a beachhead on the ego-mainland that is a more satisfactory living space than any of the islands, and at the same time make friends with the animals, the instincts, in the unconscious. That is what can happen, through projection, in the analytic relationship.

---

[3] "The Psychology of the Transference," *The Practice of Psychotherapy*, CW 16, par. 374.

As a general rule the unconscious first appears in projected form. In analysis this is called transference: the analysand's beachhead, the still-unconscious healing "answer," is projected onto the analyst, whose response is called the countertransference. It's a set-up. The analyst knows both that he is expected to heal and that he cannot. More: he can be tricked into believing he can.

The transference is as many-headed as the mythical Hydra and has as many arms as an octopus. The analyst parries its blows while he waits for the healing factor to constellate in the analysand.

How this happens, if and when it does, has given rise to speculation about a wounded healer archetype, a dynamic presumed to be at work in any therapeutic relationship. The name derives from the legend of Asclepius, a famous Greek doctor who in recognition of his own wounds set up a sanctuary where others could come to be healed of theirs.

Those seeking to be cured went through a process called incubation. First they had a cleansing bath. This was thought to have a purifying effect on the soul as well as the body. Uncontaminated by the body, the soul was free to commune with the god. After some preliminary sacrificial offerings, the incubants lay on a couch—Greek *cline*, whence derives the name for our modern clinics—and went to sleep. If they were lucky, they had a healing dream and woke up feeling great. If they were luckier, a snake came in the night and bit them.[4]

The use of a couch in classical Freudian analysis stems from this ancient practice. Few Jungians use a couch, preferring to sit face to face, but it sometimes appears symbolically in the preamble to dreams ("I am lying on a couch . . .") to indicate that the unconscious has been activated.

The wounded healer archetype can be schematized by the same "cross-cousin marriage" diagram used by Jung to illustrate the many

---

[4] *The Greek Myths*, vol. 1 (Harmondsworth: Pelican Books, 1955), pp. 173-177. See also C.A. Meier, *Ancient Incubation and Modern Psychotherapy* (Evanston, IL: Northwestern University Press, 1967).

lines of communication in any relationship.[5] Only the names are different.

The drawing below shows six double-headed arrows, indicating that communication moves in both directions. That makes twelve ways in which information can pass between analyst and analysand. Add one more, the completely unexpected, for a baker's dozen.

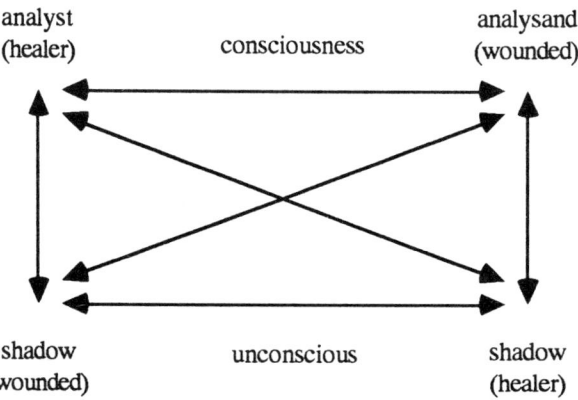

According to this paradigm, although the analyst is presumed to have become somewhat conscious of his own wounds—through a lengthy personal analysis—they still live a shadowy existence. Which is to say, they don't hurt so much, but they can always be reconstellated by phantoms from the past or by contact with someone whose wounds are similar.

Enter the analysand on his knees, hurting but not knowing why. His inner healer is in his shadow, potentially available. Various dialogues take place, one at a time or simultaneously, as shown by the diagram. The analysand's wounds are transferred through the unconscious onto the analyst, who experiences, say, a knot in the stomach. The analyst reacts to this, identifies the wounds and at-

---

[5] "The Psychology of the Transference," *The Practice of Psychotherapy,* CW 16, par. 422. See also my *Survival Papers,* p 73.

tempts to reach a conscious understanding of them. In one way or another the analyst's awareness is passed back to the analysand.

That's what's supposed to happen, and sometimes it does. But it might take years.

In this model, the unconscious relationship between analyst and analysand is quite as important, in terms of the healing process, as what is actually said—and perhaps even more so.[6] As James Hillman points out:

> In an analysis, the intimacy grows between two people less through the horizontal connection than through the parallel vertical connections of each within himself. Each listens as much to the effect of the other within and to these inner reactions as to the other. Each takes the other in.[7]

The implications of all this are twofold:

1) Healing can take place only if the analyst has an ongoing relationship with the unconscious, that is, stays aware of his shadowy wounds. Otherwise he identifies with the healer—that's a form of inflation—and they're both in the soup.

2) Depth psychology is a dangerous profession. An analyst is ever prone to being infected by the other's wounds. This happens when you takes on somebody else's problems as if they were your own. There's a thin line between empathy and identification, hence the high incidence of depression and even suicide among those in the so-called helping professions.

It is now well known that analysis is not a panacea, that some people do not "improve" or "get better," no matter how much analysis they have. The mystery is what happens when it works, why some people actually benefit from it. The wounded healer concept, for want of a better, makes sense to me.

*

---

[6] See C. Jess Groesbeck, "The Archetypal Image of the Wounded Healer," *Journal of Analytical Psychology,* vol. 20, no. 2 (July 1975), pp. 122-144.
[7] *Insearch* (New York: Charles Scribner's Sons, 1967), p.38.

Norman has been at this for over a year. He came for the right reason—he had nowhere else to go. He knows in his head that analysis is open-ended, it's not like going to a doctor for a quick fix, a pill to kill the pain. However, he'd still like to get it over with, be "cured." He doesn't yet realize that it will never be over, that he'll always be up against himself.

Over time you can establish a few beachheads, but there are still all those other islands.

2
Norman Takes a Flyer

Any human experience may be a maze in which to wander to destruction or a laboratory for the creation of consciousness, depending upon the way it is met.
—Eleanor Bertine, *Human Relationships.*

Norman wandered in ten minutes late and fidgeted for another five. We made small talk.

"I hurt," said Norman finally. "I wake up in the morning feeling miserable. I put in time at the office feeling awful and I go to bed feeling wretched. What kind of life is that?"

I rolled a cigarette and watched Norman pace.

He picked among the things on my bookcase—a diamond-eyed snake wrapped around a crystal, a box of rings, some colored glass stones, a badge promoting Princeton books *(Jung at Heart)*, a tiny sculpted woman I traded years ago for a few hours of analysis. I'll not do that again. The sculpture works, the analysis didn't.

Norman looked out the window and sighed.

"I do a great job," he said. "Sales in my area have doubled in the past two years. I meet the quotas they set and they raise them. I meet those and they raise them again. I don't mind that at all. It's a great challenge."

I waited.

"But it has no meaning."

This was the first time in our hours together that Norman had said the magic word. I wanted to hug him.

"It pays the bills," I remarked.

"Yes," said Norman, "but what about *my* bills? I've been thinking lately about possibilities. I'm restless. I'm drawn to travel posters like a magnet. I have a yen to get away. Maybe I need a change."

I had suggested something similar to Norman not too long ago. Now I devilishly advocated the opposite.

"What about the here and now, your responsibilities?" I asked. I peered at him over my glasses. "Your children?"

Norman shrugged.

"I also have responsibilities to myself," he said. "I'm in a rut. Every day is the same. I go through the motions. I do my job and I feel empty. It's getting me down."

I nodded.

"I dreamt about my brother last night," said Norman. "He waved to me from an airplane. I was hopping along the ground on a pogo stick.

" 'Come fly with me!' he called."

"Your brother?" I didn't recall this sibling.

"Yes," said Norman, looking at me. "He's an engineer, a troubleshooter for an oil company. He goes all over the world. He's full of ideas and loves to party."

Never mind, said Rachel, you can't remember everything.

"Bill is three years older than me," Norman continued. "When I was a baby—our mother says—he'd pass my crib and give me a smack. I don't recall that but I remember him taunting me when no one was watching. When I was eight we got boxing gloves and he beat me black and blue. I fought back the tears but in the end I went bawling to mom. Bill got a good licking. He left me alone after that. As teenagers we were always competing, but we got along okay."

Norman grinned. "He was stronger but I was smarter."

They were lucky. There are brothers who tear each other apart. It's a powerful archetypal motif. You see it in the Biblical story of Cain and Abel; in Egyptian mythology there's Horus and Set. Psychologically, it's a well-documented phenomenon. In Freudian terminology it falls under the heading of sibling rivalry. In the Jungian model, it has to do with the conflict between ego and shadow.[1] Occasionally they may collude, but mostly they're at odds.

---

[1] See *The Survival Papers,* chapter 4, "The Hero's Journey."

"He's the jock ," said Norman, "and I'm the egg-head."

The world's oldest surviving myth, the Gilgamesh Epic, is about two brothers. It's not well known, even among educated people. I never heard of it before I went to Zurich.

Gilgamesh was a young Sumerian ruler, half man and half god, who after many heroic exploits became too big for his boots. He was proud and arrogant and tyrannized his subjects. The gods sent down a brother, Enkidu, to take him down a peg.

Enkidu was an animal-man. His whole body was covered with hair. At first he roamed the plains, wild, living close to nature. He was all animal until a woman dragged him into the bush and tore off his pelt; then he became half man, familiar to lust.

Enkidu and Gilgamesh tangled at the temple gates. It was a long and nasty battle. They fought tooth and nail, but it was a stand-off in the end. They finally embraced and became best buddies. Together they were half man, a quarter god and a quarter animal.

For years Gilgamesh and Enkidu traveled the world defeating awesome monsters like Humbaba, minion of the Great Mother Ishtar and guardian of the cedar forest, and the bull of heaven, a fearsome beast who killed hundreds with a single snort. The bull of heaven had been created by the gods at Ishtar's request, to destroy Gilgamesh because he refused to service her. It didn't work.

Then Enkidu got sick and died. That was the decree of the gods, to placate Ishtar. That's the thing about gods—what they give one day, they can take away the next.

Gilgamesh was bereft. His quest thereafter was for the elixir of life. He found it in the shape of a thorny plant at the bottom of the sea. Joyfully he set off for home. But one day, as he was taking a cold bath, a snake ate the plant. Thus snakes gained the power to shed their old skin and thereby renew their life. Poor Gilgamesh gnashed his teeth and wept bitterly. He had it and he lost it! He slunk home a chastened man and died of gout.

All that was chiseled in stone. Seven thousand years ago!

Meanwhile, Norman was chewing his nails.

"I'm bored," he said, averting his eyes.

And well he might. A few sessions back I had pointed out that boredom is a symptom of inflation. Weary with the world, as if one has seen everything and knows it all. That's god-like.

I didn't feel holier than Norman. I've been there myself often enough. So has Arnold. Just the other day, over a pint, he confided a similar malaise.

"Wouldn't it be nice," he said, "to be *surprised?*"

I knew what he meant. Arnold knew I knew what he meant. I knew that Arnold knew I knew what he meant.

I was bored too.

Boredom isn't all bad. Sometimes it's the only thing that'll get me off my butt. If I get bored enough, fed up with things as they are, maybe I'll do something about it. But for that to happen, I need my shadow.

Like Jung, I see inflation as a regression of consciousness into the unconscious.[2] The flow of energy toward the unconscious constellates the shadow, that side of myself I'm not normally aware of. And so when I'm bored I wander about, noting what catches my interest. In short, I follow my energy. It's time-consuming, and where the energy wants to go often raises ethical questions. But it does away with boredom.

Astrologers might attribute this state of mind to the fact that I'm a Capricorn, an earth sign. Henry Miller was a Capricorn, and so was that rogue Richard Nixon. Capricorns are ruled by Saturn, a very heavy planet. In alchemy Saturn is associated with lead, in psychology with depression and negative thinking. Astrologically, Capricorns are weighted down. Unable to fly, they get stuck in routine. Hence the feeling of boredom.

I believe there is some truth in astrology and I like the symbolism. But in coming to grips with myself I find Jung's model of typology more helpful.

Take Arnold and me, for instance. Typologically, we are opposites. My best functions are probably sensation and thinking. Arnold

---

[2] See below, p. 126.

is highly intuitive and his feeling function is quite acute. He usually knows what something's worth to him. I often don't know how I feel about anything. To the extent that we function differently, Arnold and I are shadow brothers.

The shadow is like a mirror that shows you an unfamiliar face—a person you don't see as yourself, but under certain circumstances could be.

Before I met Arnold, my boredom was a bottomless pit. Left to myself, I have no imagination. Sure, Arnold gets bored, but with him it's a momentary thing. Arnold lives in a world of possibilities. I don't, unless I'm tired or have had a few drinks. In that state—Jung called it an *abaissement du niveau mental*, a lowering of the level of consciousness[3]—I'm besieged by what might be. Arnold is like that all the time, sober.

Arnold is always coming up with something new. The Arnolds of this world, if introverted, build better mouse-traps. As extraverts, they sell them to cats.

Arnold's way of looking at things has often pulled me out of a rut. At the same time, I get anxious just listening to him talk. That's because my intuition tends to be morbid. I fasten on the negative possibilities—everything that could go wrong.

Of course, intuitives have shadows too. When *their* level of consciousness is lowered, they get compulsive about detail. That's what inferior sensation looks like.

It's a psychological fact: the way we usually aren't is dormant in the unconscious. At first it may seem unacceptable, even ugly, the last thing we need. But the more we resist that other side, the more negative it becomes.

Marie-Louise von Franz describes this phenomenon in the two attitude types:

> The inferior function tends to have, in its negative aspect, a barbaric character. It can cause a state of possession: if, for example, intro-

---

[3] "Concerning Rebirth," *The Archetypes and the Collective Unconscious*, CW 9i, pars. 213ff.

verts fall into extraversion, they do so in a possessed and barbaric way. I mean barbaric in the sense of being unable to exert conscious control, being swept away, being unable to put a brake on, unable to stop. This kind of exaggerated, driven extraversion is rarely found in genuine extraverts, but in introverts it can be like a car without brakes that speeds on without the slightest control. . . . Such inferior extraversion may suddenly pop out in this way when an introvert is drunk.[4]

Similarly, a sensation type can be possessed by intuition and a feeling type by thinking—and vice versa.

According to Jung's model of the psyche, the opposite is always waiting in the wings. Drunk or sober, the shadow will out. The only question is whether you're aware of it or not.

Personally, I am at home with physical reality and the immediate tasks at hand. I love routine and familiar surroundings. You can't pull the wool over my eyes when it comes to the five senses. No sir. Typologically this is associated with a good sensation function.

I see an aspect of myself in Norman.

An aspect, said Rachel, that's a laugh.

Norman's mainstay is his sensation function, only he's not quite as introverted as I am. Norman doesn't mind traveling, it goes with his job. I actively avoid leaving my house; it takes all I've got to go to the corner store for a loaf of bread.

Typologically, Norman has a *shadowy* capacity for adventure. He would have gone abroad long before this, only it never occurred to him. He has hewed to the straight and narrow—well, geographically—more or less oblivious to possibilities.

Meanwhile, his brother Bill, who from Norman's account is an extraverted intuitive, has all the fun. Or so Norman thinks.

Bill is Norman's Arnold.

Whereas intuitives tend to be tripped up by what's right under their noses—practical details—Norman and I are both apt to be se-

---

[4] *Jung's Typology* (Zurich: Spring Publications, 1971), p. 55. See also my *Personality Types: Jung's Model of Typology* (Toronto: Inner City Books, 1987), pp. 25-31.

duced by possibilities. In me as in Norman, this manifests as boredom, a vague unease, a nameless dissatisfaction with things as they are. When I feel that way, I know something's brewing. I pay attention because in my experience it means I'm unbalanced. My shadow too wants to live.

Last year, for instance, Arnold told me about an old mill in the country he was thinking of buying. He was fed up with the city, he said, and wanted to move. He described the mill and surrounding hills and what it would be like to live there.

"It's unique," he enthused, showing me a picture. "There's space. I could do a lot with it."

I was immediately on the defensive. I'd put a lot of time and energy into my house. It was just the way I wanted it. I had no conscious desire to move. But as I listened to Arnold a longing for the country crept over me. Is that where my energy wants to go, I thought. I tried to stay alert.

"When you have everything you want," said Arnold, "what else is there?"

"Women?" I ventured. "Fast cars?"

"Nature," replied Arnold. "The answer lies in the soil."

He handed me a sheaf of real estate listings. "Think about Jung's tower in Bollingen," he said. "Create something new. Expand!"

The next few weeks were difficult.

I viewed some country properties and tried to imagine owning one. I saw magnificent estates with ponds, orchards, barns and even good ski runs. I trekked through the woods with a bird book and ate wild berries. It took a lot of time and it left me cold.

"Live here," pressed Arnold. "You'll get used to it. You need a slower pace."

There was something in that but not enough to budge me.

The truth is, I'm a bit wary of nature due to my mother complex. This may seem a far-fetched connection, but for some years I have not been able to separate the out-of-doors from the Great Mother. It's like quicksand for me. I don't know, maybe that's why I don't like going to the corner store for bread.

I think it started in Zurich after I had been on a day-long hike in the hills. The house I shared with Arnold was in a small village, an area of great natural beauty. The foothills to the Swiss Alps were right outside. I would often set out in the early morning and not return till late afternoon.

I described it to my analyst: the sun sparkling on the snowy peaks, the wildflowers, the small animals starting in the brush, the deep refreshing silence barely disturbed by bird calls and the occasional staff-toting Teuton.

"It's a wonderful experience, I feel at one."

He raised his eyebrows.

Eeee, what next.

"At . . . one," he said, slowly rolling the words. "What exactly does that mean?"

"Peace," I replied gamely. "No conflict, no pain."

He nodded. "I see. Swallowed by the great maw."

That's what he said, this man who stopped practicing every summer and holed up in a remote log cabin with no electricity, no running water, no toilet. Shit, I was only walking in the woods!

I became quite agitated. Tears came to my eyes. "I feel really good out there. You're so suspicious! Can't I do anything right?"

He smiled. "You feel good just being. It relieves you of the responsibility of doing."

Well now. I had been reading about how important it was for men to just be—archetypally a feminine mode of functioning—instead of getting caught up in their usual goal-oriented activities. I was doing my bit, and I said so.

"That's true," my analyst agreed, "when a man identifies with the traditional masculine model. Then he needs the opposite. But you have quite enough of the feminine, don't you think?"

Since then I have shunned country hikes and done a great deal. I am now at the point where nature poses no real threat; it might even be seen as a reward. Still.

Meanwhile, Arnold fell out of love with the old mill and found something he liked better.

"Forty acres, a choice view and its own swimming hole!" He rubbed his hands.

This too died a natural death. And the next, and the next.

I finally put it to him: "Are you moving or not? What are your actual intentions?"

By then I had figured out that the only motivation for me to move to the country was to be near him.

Arnold shrugged. "It's always a possibility."

I can make some sense of our relationship in terms of Gilgamesh and Enkidu. But sometimes it's hard to tell who's Gilgamesh and who's Enkidu. It all depends on the time of day, the weather and what's in the mail-box. Jointly, we have the elixir of life. Left to ourselves, we both thirst for more. And there's always that snake.

I am grateful for my association with Arnold. I used to think there was no life outside the present, only speculation by insurance companies. Now I know there's something else.

I turned my attention to Norman. He was staring at the wall, morose. Where does his energy want to go, I thought. What is it, right now, that represents his natural urge for life?

"I've never been abroad," said Norman, "have you?"

There it was. That's one of the pitfalls of being an analyst. Sometimes you think so hard you miss the obvious.

"Yes, I've traveled," I said.

Norman opened his notebook. "Here's a dream. I'm in a strange town, trying to get home. I'm standing on a corner with my briefcase. A police car is watching me. I'm peeing down my leg, hoping the police don't see it. How about that?"

"What are your associations to peeing?"

"I think of aiming down the side of the toilet so no one will hear me. I don't know what women do."

We laughed.

"And police?" I asked.

"Well, they protect you. Or sometimes they prevent you from doing what you want."

"Peeing is a natural process," I said. "Urine is a waste product. You can't hold it in indefinitely. That points to something you have to get rid of. In alchemy the urine of an uncorrupted boy figures as a solvent, psychologically related to the naive and spontaneous attitudes associated with childhood."

An uncorrupted boy? said Rachel. Puer, for short, I said.

I thought out loud. "What are you holding in? A childish attitude that doesn't work, maybe? What is it you don't want the police—your conscience, perhaps—to know about?"

"It's a mystery to me," said Norman, "unless . . . well, what if I wanted to keep something from Nancy? What if *she's* my conscience?"

I agreed it was a possibility.

Norman turned a page. "Here's another one. I'm in a department store, late at night. I'm trying to escape from a woman dressed in red. In one hand she has a whip. In the other there's a cage. She starts after me, I take off barefoot, sprinting through the crowd. I'm terrified. If she catches me, I've had it."

Department stores in dreams point to a collective attitude, like buses, trains and office buildings. The woman in red is a symbol of the devouring mother. She's out to whip him into shape. She'd cage him, put him in a traveling circus and charge admission.

I thought of the writer Franz Kafka, whose mother complex dwarfed Norman's. Kafka had a problem living out his sexuality. For years he dithered between having a close relationship with a woman and his need for privacy.

Meanwhile, his anima became impatient. Indeed, rapacious. He described her like this:

> "No, let me alone! No, let me alone!" I shouted without pause all the way along the streets, and again and again she laid hold of me, again and again the clawed hands of the siren struck at my breast from the side or across my shoulder.[5]

---

[5] *The Diaries of Franz Kafka,* 1914-1923, trans. Martin Greenberg, ed. Max Brod (London: Secker & Warburg, 1949), p. 182. I have commented more

I eyed Norman. Siren, mother, it comes to the same thing. Norman is inclined to project this virago onto his wife. She's in himself, of course. And yes, if she catches him he's had it.

We shook hands at the door. I held Norman back. I wanted to encourage his energy without directing it.

"Travel," I said. "Not a bad idea. No harm in looking into it."

---

extensively on the role of the mother complex in Kafka's psychology in *The Secret Raven: Conflict and Transformation* (Toronto: Inner City Books, 1980).

3
Dear Gladys

Every society is characterized by a certain level of individuation beyond which the normal individual cannot go.
—Erich Fromm, *Fear of Freedom.*

Travel broadens the mind.
—Anonymous.

A month later Norman announced he was taking a leave of absence. He had talked to his boss and they could fill in for a few weeks. He had booked a flight to Paris.

I was glad to hear it. As a matter of fact, I could use his hours working on myself.

"Last night I lay in bed drawing views of my penis," said Norman. "First limp, then erect. I labeled them My Cock In The Night, 1 and 2. It was very satisfying."

We stirred the caldron awhile. It isn't only witches who get to do that. There are warlocks too.

"Can you afford the time off?" I asked.

Norman shifted in his chair.

"I'll make do with less," he said.

That expression triggered some memories. I was in an unusual mood that day. I'd been working on material that brought up the past. I had an impulse to tell Norman something of myself.

I imagined rolling up my sleeves and giving him back his check. "Here," I'd say, "this one's on me."

A handsome gesture, said Rachel, but rather narcissistic. What about the transference?

Good point. Norman was still embedded in his own life. My story would be intrusive.

For the rest of the hour we explored the symbolism in Norman's dreams. Thank heaven he had some. I am quite lost without these nightly commentaries on daily life. Without dreams there are only opinions.

That's one of the major differences between analysis and therapy. Therapy is generally supportive, it focuses on building up ego strength. Analysis is a disciplined process that is only appropriate—or indeed possible—with an already well-developed ego. Analysis depends on messages from the unconscious to balance conscious attitudes. Dreams are the primary source of information for what's going on down there.

We saw nothing in Norman's material to suggest he was on the wrong track. I wished him a good holiday and closed the door.

Now, said Rachel, roll up your sleeves.

*

Many years ago, when I was twenty-three, I had a regular job. I was what they called a junior executive and I had a lot of responsibility. I'd been recruited out of university to do public relations work for a large consumer goods company.

"Security," they said, pointing out their many products: soap, toothpaste, cake-mix, nut-oil, strawberry conserve, beef sausages, fish fingers, oleo margarine, maple syrup, peanut butter, etc.

They flew me down to Cleveland to meet the top brass.

"Personal hygiene and food," they said. "People will always eat. They may not wash but even in a depression people gotta eat."

The people in the company were all very friendly. We called each other by our first names and higher management ate with us in the staff canteen.

My job was to placate irate customers and make them feel important. They put me in a room with my name on the door and gave me a personal secretary. All the letters of complaint came to me. There were a lot. I sat in a swivel chair with my feet on the desk and dictated answers.

44 Dear Gladys

"Gladys, take a letter."

Gladys was my secretary. She was a perky little thing with a silver button in one ear.

"Dear Mr. Bell. Thank you for your recent letter period. We are most surprised to learn that unlike many thousands of satisfied Whitey Toothpaste users comma your teeth have turned black period. Although laboratory tests have proved the Whitey whiteness claims comma, it is just possible that in your case the effect may not be as immediate as with others period.

"Or as bad."

Gladys giggled. Dear Gladys, she thought I was a hoot.

"New paragraph. Ahhh, nevertheless comma, true to our promise, we herewith refund your money plus postage and two free giant-size Whiteys period. We hope that you will persevere comma, proving for yourself that Whitey Toothpaste really does make teeth whiter period. Yours sincerely etc.

"There are more of those, Gladys. Send a copy to Quality Control, with a memo. Whose teeth are you using down there?

"Say Gladys, where's that report on skin eruptions? Call Dave Stephens at the *Telegram*. Tell him I've been called away on important business. Tell him, uh, the company's lawyers are looking into these complaints with a view to settling out of court in case their truth in substance is established, which we do not of course admit. Send another memo to Quality Control. What are you doing to the Bunny Flakes? The old man is on to this. It could be your skin next.

"Gladys, take a letter.

"Dear Mr. Appleby. We are sorry indeed to hear of the distress you experienced through the use of our product comma, Mother Maxwell's Quick-Make Bicky-Mix period. I assure you it is not usual to find a mouse in it period. Our Bicky-Mix foreman attributes this to the playful nature of some of our more junior employees comma, who will nevertheless be duly disciplined period.

"New paragraph. Under separate cover we are sending you one dozen packs of Mother Maxwell's Quick-Make Bicky-Mix comma of assorted kinds period. We hope you will continue to inform us of any irregularities in our products that come to your attention period. Quality Control comma Mr. Appleby comma is an everyday concern here period. Yours etc.

"Gladys, inform Shipping to stand by with more gift cartons. The little buggers are at it again."

That's the way it went. Sand in the talcum powder, mice in the cake mix, hair in the jam.

Gladys would punch out the letters on a tape and run off a few dozen copies on an electric typewriter that made them look individually typed. That was part of the game. I didn't think twice about it. Bound to be some problems in a company that size. Somebody had to answer the letters.

I was making decent money. They said I had the right stuff and would move up through the ranks. I lived in a large bachelor flat with modern furniture and a hi-fi set. I had a two-year-old Dodge and a hand-made suit that cost $120. I looked very impressive in midnight blue. I got my hair cut every Thursday and used Wild Root Cream-Oil to keep it neat. On payday I had a shoe-shine for a quarter. "Here," I'd say, adding a nickel, "keep the change."

I was captain of the bowling team. I had three cameras. I took pictures of factory workers and edited *Sparkles,* the company magazine. After work I played softball and drank beer with the boys.

I was doing what my education had prepared me for. Others of my age were climbing mountains, exploring jungles, roaming around Europe. I didn't envy them. Why would I? They were shirking the duties of real life. They had no place in society; I was a valuable member of the community.

I was an organization man and I liked it.

However, after awhile I became uneasy and I didn't know why. I talked to Arnold about it.

Hold on, said Rachel, this happened many years before you knew Arnold.

Thank you, so it did.

It was Walt I talked to. Walt was a stringer for Reuters wire service. He lived in a room in a college frat house because it was cheap.

We'd studied journalism together. Walt had dreams of being a foreign correspondent in Karachi. Reuters put him on something called pig stocks.

"Walt," I said, helping myself to a beer and some Cheese-Whiz, "I'm uneasy and I don't know why."

Walt reclined in a dentist's chair he'd picked up in a garage sale. He cradled a bottle and chewed gum with his mouth open. He was holding a copy of *Submariner,* a comic book he favored. A dusty fan ticked overhead. Dirty clothes were piled in a corner. Dishes were stacked in the sink and the radio didn't work. A display window dummy, dressed in pink pyjamas, was propped against one wall. Dozens of egg cartons, painted bright yellow, had been stapled to the ceiling. Walt told me they were good insulation against noise. The yellow was for looks. The room was divided by a wooden trestle with the stenciled words, Caution—Men At Work.

I was not taken with Walt's way of life, but he saw things in a way I didn't. Maybe that's why I confused him with Arnold.

I made myself a sweet onion sandwich and downed a few olives. "I have a job that many guys would give their eye teeth for," I said. "I worked my ass off to get it. My family is proud of me. Why doesn't it feel right?"

Walt shrugged. Most of my peers envied me. They clapped me on the back and said I was a leader among men. But Walt was not impressed.

"Your life is taken up with cruddy minutiae," he said. "Your work has no meaning."

"What I do is a great help to many people," I said defensively.

I was annoyed. Walt would borrow money from me but he didn't respect what I did to earn it. Sure, I could laugh about it with Gladys, but that was between us, in-house talk. I was actually very proud of my job.

Walt took a swig and scratched his belly. He was short and fat. His head was shaved bald. He wore a t-shirt, torn and stained. With high cheekbones, thick sensuous lips and a jutting forehead, he looked a lot like Neanderthal Man.

Walt was a slob, pure and simple. He had no persona to speak of; what you saw was what you got. He mocked organized society and tolerated no pretensions. He was forever exposing the banalities of polite conversation.

"Yes," I would agree, "The expression 'How are you?' means nothing. But it breaks the ice."

"I hear you," he'd say, fingering his pate. "I just don't like ice."

When he wasn't filing stories for Reuters Walt hung out in The Black Bull, a tavern with seven pool tables. He played poker and shot craps with the locals. He drank a lot and fell down stairs. I could never understand why some women liked him. My girlfriend thought he was obnoxious. She refused to have anything to do with him because he stuck his finger in her pimples.

Walt and I were as different as night and day. I lived on the surface, all show. Walt lived out of his gut, close to the ground. I was always a bit afraid of him because he didn't live by my rules. However, he took me to Hungarian weddings, where I danced all night and went around saying, "Yaksamiyish!" I wasn't sure what that meant but it made me feel happy.

Once I took Walt to a luncheon meeting of the Industrial Editors' Association. I coached him beforehand on how to behave.

"Don't drink too much," I pleaded. "They know me here."

Walt was fine until the head speaker, already swaying after four martinis, suddenly stopped in mid-sentence. He went all white, put a hand to his mouth and threw up between his fingers. Walt was uncontrollable after that.

Now I said: "My company makes everything under the sun. Without it the world would be a sorrier place."

Walt belched. "And what would you be without the company?"

I had no answer for that. Such a question had never occurred to me. I had been groomed for a world where the road to success was paved with ten million best-selling copies of Dale Carnegie's *How To Win Friends and Influence People*. That was my life and I knew no other. I won't say it's what I had in mind when I went into the world to make my mark, but I had everything I wanted.

"I have everything I want," I said, chewing on a bunch of dried Chinese noodles.

That was one thing about Walt. He never cooked a decent meal but he always had great snack food.

"So why are you uneasy?" said Walt.

"That's what I asked you in the first place," I said, savoring a pickled kipper.

"What about those books you were going to write?" said Walt.

I munched an oyster on a Ritz biscuit. Yes, I had dim memories of wanting to be an author. Like almost everyone else in our class I had dreamed of writing The Great Canadian Novel.

"That wasn't the real world."

"Reality is what you make it," said Walt.

He heaved out of the dentist's chair and tossed his cigarette in the sink. "Look, go eat in a restaurant, I'm expecting a chick."

Walt's words haunted me.

I thought about my earlier ambitions. I started reading again: Thomas Wolfe, Hemingway, Steinbeck, Scott Fitzgerald, Kerouac, Ferlinghetti, Allen Ginsberg. I became more and more dissatisfied. I no longer enjoyed photo jaunts to the factory. I missed important meetings. I took long wet lunch breaks and left work early to play snooker with Walt. He taught me which color came next and how to put English on the cue ball. I took flute lessons instead of boning up on new brand names. My bowling average dropped.

I had a bad case of itchy feet.

It finally came down to buying a 1956 Thunderbird convertible with the thousand dollars I'd saved or going to Europe. A thousand dollars went a long way in those days.

For a few weeks it was a toss-up, but in the end I opted for Europe. That's how I became a struggling writer.

The young guys at work understood why I left. Those who were firmly ensconced didn't. Jim Weathers, the advertising manager, dropped into my office. He was a ten-year man.

"Hear you're leaving us."

"That's right." I smiled. "Time to try something different."

"You've been here, what, two years now?"

"That's right."

"You won't get your profit-sharing bonuses."

I shrugged.

Jim went to the window, chewing the stub of a pencil. I knew what was coming next.

"You want more money, is that it?"

"No."

"You don't think there's a future here for you?"

"I know there is, that's what I'm afraid of."

Jim was only the advance guard. Over the next few weeks they popped in and out, one after the other, offering condolences, paying their last respects.

"Always a place here for a bright boy."

"You were going places."

"You'll lose your pension rights."

They looked at me as if I had some loathesome disease. And who was to say it might not be catching? It reminded me of the way married couples react when they hear of partners who've split up. They close ranks, like mourners at a funeral, viewing the remains.

There were others. Relatives, friends of the family, neighbors, people I once knew at school. At odd hours they came, accosted me in the street. They sent little notes expressing dismay. They who hardly knew me.

"Come back and be one of us," they said.

They made it damn hard to leave.

My boss took me out for lunch. We sat around his club smoking expensive cigars while he gave me a lecture on affluence—why not to be cynical about it.

"You'll always regret leaving, son," he said. "You'll never get a better job."

"You've been very understanding, Mr. Jones," I said earnestly.

I rather liked the old guy. He was a great talker, a born salesman. Ask him what time it was and he'd tell you how to make a watch. *He* could sell mouse-traps to cats. His hair was steely grey and one leg was shorter than the other. He'd been with the company for thirty-five years and loved it.

"I'm still young," I said. "There's lots of time. I hope one day you'll be proud of me."

Before leaving I was asked to recommend someone for my position. I told them Walt would be an excellent choice.

"You think he's executive material?"

"He's just the man," I said with conviction.

I thought it was a huge joke, but Walt was offered the job. And he took it.

I had a friend whose dad owned a cargo plane. He had a contract to fly rhesus monkeys from India to Canada for use in medical research. He said he could get me on a flight to London, where the plane stopped on the way back. And so, one dark night, as rain fell, I slung my bag into the hold of a decrepit DC-3.

The flight took twenty-four hours. We droned over the Atlantic at 6,000 feet. There were two bucket seats for passengers and a lot of empty cages. An Indian boy named Roger sat beside me. He was the company agent. Every few hours he took a bag of sandwiches from his battered suitcase and shared them out.

"Hey boy," said Roger. He'd done this run many times. "You don't want to be on this kite when it's loaded with monkeys."

"Oh?" I was watching the ocean liners far below. They would take five or six days.

"Monkeys don't like heights," said Roger. "They shit and piss and throw up."

"I can imagine."

The sensation of being free was very strong that night. Free from a lot of dross. My heart was full. I was really looking forward to being somebody else.

"You got no idea. Once we hit an air pocket and the plane dropped 500 feet. All that shit and monkey vomit spilled out of the cages and there I was in the middle of it. I tell you I was sick, boy."

"That must have been awful."

I didn't know what was in store for me, but I wasn't sorry I'd left. I wondered about Walt, though.

"Sheer terror," said Roger.

Walt and I kept in touch for awhile. A few months later he sacked Gladys and hired a new secretary, an eighteen-year-old named Marilyn. She couldn't type but that didn't bother Walt. ("I give her lessons evenings and she's coming on a treat.") His attitude toward corporate life didn't change, but he turned out some presentable issues of *Sparkles*.

After a year we stopped writing. I was making new friends, learning new ways to survive. I didn't think about Walt until one day I got a letter postmarked Venice West, California.

"Dear pal. Some weeks ago, in a fit of stark clarity of mind, and finding myself several hundreds of dollars in debt—the vagaries of Dame Chance—I did a midnight flit. Imperial Oil, unbeknownst to them, paid for the trip. This will be knownst to them soon enough, when their marvellous IBM machines get to work on the credit card receipts.

"I took Marilyn with me. We had an argument passing through Wichita and I"m sorry to say I turfed her out. She might have been able to get a job here, which I can't because I don't have a Social Security Number.

"In Venice you can sleep on the beach. You should see all the phonies and fakes. Yes, they're all here, Earl the Pearl, Big John, Fag Ten, a whole profusion of dykes and pimps. Every few minutes there are things that come out of the water and fling themselves on the beach. These things are called breakers. I sit and watch them for hours. Even God wastes a lot of energy.

"I am writing a book and am on page 80. The trouble is, I have exactly 25 cents to my name and I have the runs from cheap wine. For a week I've eaten nothing but tinned peas.

"Pray for me, there's a new dawn acomin'. Do you know what happens to people who fail to file an income tax return?"

With mixed feelings I sent Walt an American Express traveler's check for $20.

Meanwhile, I was living in London, off Sloane Square in the heart of Chelsea. I was having a ball. Theater, opera, dance, it was all there. After seeing a performance I got so excited wandering the foggy London streets that I often stood motionless, waiting for someone to appear, a giant perhaps, who'd shout, "STOP! Stop enjoying yourself! It's not allowed."

I was not psychologically minded in those days and I didn't dream, but I knew how I felt.

I shared a large apartment with three other men. We were a motley crew: Mike, engineer with Air-Vent International; tall, handsome, a clean-cut profile, superbly filling his athletic supporter. Harry, self-confessed intellectual, a former civil servant from Duluth, Minnesota, teaching English to foreign students in Clapham Junction. Irving, short and dumpy with a Vandyke beard, foreign correspondent for the *Lethbridge Herald*, devoted fan of Lewis Carroll.

And me, ex-organization man, looking for something else, learning what life is like off the ladder.

I was making ends meet by teaching in Secondary Modern Schools, the low end of the English education system. There was a shortage of teachers in England so it wasn't hard to get work. Especially in Battersea and Wandsworth, where classroom riots were the norm and canes were standard issue.

Writing was my life. And reading. With Harry's coaching I graduated from American novels to what he called the modern European mind. Harry's attitude to writing was uncompromising.

"The clever, the popular and the merely adequate," said Harry, "are a waste of time."

He read me his credo, a passage from Cyril Connolly's book, *The Unquiet Grave:* "Writers engrossed in any literary task which is not an assault on perfection are their own dupes. Every line that doesn't tend in that direction is pointless and the writer might as well be peeling potatoes."

To further my education Harry recommended some serious writers, like Samuel Beckett, Kafka, Rilke, Nietzsche, Kierkegaard, Celine, René Daumal, Heidegger, Sartre, Dostoyevski, Pirandello and yes, old C.G. Jung himself. Most of them I'd never heard of. I read them all, one by one. They blew my mind.

Irving, a self-made journalist, had quite different ideas. His hero was Hemingway.

"Shallow," said Harry, "no echoing depths." And he would cite a passage from, say, Kafka's *Castle*.

"What's an echoing depth?" asked Mike. His reading was confined to Agatha Christie and blueprints.

"It's what you thrill to," said Harry.

"It may thrill you," said Irving. "It depresses me."

"It's not enough," insisted Harry, "to tell stories."

"Me, I like a good read," observed Mike.

"These writers," said Harry, sweeping his arms wide to include all his books, "have something to say."

Irving turned up his nose. "They parade their symbolism at the reader's expense," he said. "They don't make any concessions to the common man."

"Like me," said Mike, scratching his nose.

"Nor should they," was Harry's answer. He was fond of comparing himself to Kierkegaard, who used to stand around on crowded corners so that people would think him an idler and he would escape the demoralizing effects of fame.

Harry had no ambition to write a novel. He turned out philosophical fragments, poems and symbolic monologues. Everything he wrote went into his journals. He published them some years later through a vanity press in Detroit.

For a long time Harry wouldn't show us anything. "I don't think you'd appreciate what I'm after," he said. We coaxed him and made him wash the dishes until he finally read us a few fragments. Here's a couple that turned up in his book.

> He could have led men, been cited for medals, made millions, moved mountains. But he went into the forest, straying where the trees

grew most dense. Is it any wonder he lost his way, has never been heard from since? He lay shivering in the middle of the woods because he could not remember which side of the tree the moss grew on. He died, of course, the nights were far too cold to lie about in the open. But even if he had not frozen he would have starved to death. He took no food of his own.

He could have spelled it out in so many words, left no space between the lines. He could have told the whole story from start to finish in the most realistic terms. But he refused to play second fiddle to a plot. And so he sat there, looking out to sea, playing with the tip of his iceberg, rearranging the melting surface into finely-pointed arrows, calculating, now and then, the area that lay submerged. From time to time he thought he heard the sound of breakers, but not until a small party of scouts landed a few yards away did he look up.

Harry was right. I didn't understand.

"Terrific!" I enthused, "it's coming right along."

Thank you, Dale Carnegie, said Rachel.

Mike looked blank. Irving gave Harry a hard time.

"You can write," said Irving, "but that stuff will never sell."

"So what," retorted Harry. "I'll make do with less."

"You're too bloody idealistic," said Irving. "You've got the tools but you don't know how to use them."

"You newsvendor," countered Harry. "You hack, you hawker of wares."

"Most people read to be entertained," said Irving, "not educated. They won't read you for long if you force them to think."

Harry pulled himself up to his full height, five foot six.

"I have no intention," he said, "of writing for a living."

"You want to be read, don't you? All writers do, whether they admit it or not. You can still purvey meaty thought, but you have to sugar-coat it. Look at Aldous Huxley and Sartre, even they have to cater to the masses if they want to keep eating. And your precious Nietzsche," he smiled, "would have to have a paper route to survive today."

Mike and I laughed.

"You're all fucking Philistines," said Harry with disgust.

I wasn't sure that Philistine was the right word, but fornicate we did. Several times a week we'd debouch to Finches on the Fulham Road, looking for girls. It was a favorite of ours. We loved pubs in general and this one in particular. It all happened in Finches, according to *The Daily Mirror, The News of the World* and *The Evening Standard.* And they were right. It seethed with all manner of strange folk—poets, painters, writers, actors, hangers-on.

Saturday night and the place is packed. Familiar faces of stage and screen loll against the wall. Long-faced girls, living Modigliani prints, perch on stools. Thick black eyelashes. Purple make-up. Looping Gypsy earrings. Floppy woolen sweaters. If you see it in Finches, it's in—or soon will be.

The air is thick with smoke and voices.

"Darling I'm sure we could work something out, call me at the office."

"So I said to this guy, you cunt."

"Horses, my dear, are absolutely out."

"Will it sell he said, Christ as if I cared."

"Do let me bring Akhbar, he's ever so much fun."

Irving sits in a corner miming *The Jabberwock.* Harry stands on a table, loudly reciting lines from Rilke: "Now to depart from all this incoherence that's ours, but which we can't appropriate . . . O fountain mouth, you mouth that can respond so inexhaustibly to all who ask . . ."—and one of my favorites: "Who if I cried would hear me among the angelic orders?"

On my right two smart dressers on a crawl through fashionable Chelsea are being worked over by men in beards. On my left, an American girl in horn-rimmed glasses is pumping the hand of an Indian boy.

"Gee, fancy meeting you here."

Mike and Irving approach with a girl in tow.

"This is Wendy," says Mike. "I found a toad feeling her up in the corner. I squashed him."

Mike disappears. While Irving licks Wendy's ear I flirt with her. She is Irish, four foot ten, nicely curved. Wendy is a waitress in a restaurant up the street. She's just finished her shift and is looking for bear. Her eyes twinkle.

"Do you come here often?" I ask.

Wendy smiles and rubs against my leg. She rummages in a large satchel for a pack of smokes.

"I was once goosed by Brendan Behan," she says.

It was now three o'clock in the morning. I looked at Rachel. Her eyes were slightly glazed.

"There's lots more," I said. "Wendy is a story in herself. And Irving married her!"

Rachel sniffed and said nothing. That's what she does when she thinks I've gone too far.

"I've been feeling overbalanced," I explained. "Too much senex. You know, discipline, responsibility. So the puer wants back in.[1] I could close the door, but I'd just get hammered."

Rachel accepted that.

"Did you ever regret leaving the corporate world?" she asked.

"I certainly did. For about ten minutes."

I thought of Norman. He wasn't there yet, he wouldn't resign. At this point, all he wanted was a break. Well, there were things in store for Norman that he didn't expect. That's life.

*

"Wait!" said Rachel.

I was about to close things down.

"What about Walt? What happened to him?"

I was afraid of that. Rachel doesn't miss much. I was not keen to go on with Walt's story because it wasn't a happy one. I made it short.

"Walt left Venice West because he said he felt out of place. I encouraged him to come to England but he went to Winnipeg where he

---

[1] The puer-senex polarity is discussed in *The Survival Papers,* pp. 86ff.

got a job on a newspaper. After six months he went to a radio station in Saskatoon. Then we lost touch. Three years ago I heard he was working in a meat factory in Detroit. Last year he surfaced close to home. He phoned at three in the morning to tell me I was a big cheese now so I was on his hit list. He said he would order a pile of Chinese food to be sent to my apartment unless I lent him a hundred dollars. No money, I said, send food. It never came."

I stopped.

"And?"

"There was a story in the newspaper last month," I said. "A man parked his car in a gravel pit and blew his brains out. It was Walt."

Rachel made a face.

"That's hard to believe," she said.

I agreed, but in this instance, at least, I would not tamper with the truth.

4

Enter the Dragon

An unconscious Eros always expresses itself as will to power. Women of this type, though continually "living for others," are, as a matter of fact, unable to make any real sacrifice.
—C.G. Jung, "Psychological Aspects of the Mother Archetype."

I was unprepared for Nancy's phone call. To me she was a phantom, a woman Norman married and used to live with. She had not crossed my mind since Norman left for Paris.

"I would like to make an appointment," she said.

I was not keen to see Nancy. Nor was it strictly ethical without Norman's approval.

"There are other analysts here," I said. "You'd be well served by any of them. I can recommend one."

"I want *you.*"

Oh.

Like Norman, I found it hard to say no when pressed. We fenced a little longer but I finally agreed to see her.

Nancy was a tall woman, well turned out. Rather attractive, too. There was a bit of the coquette about her. At the same time she had poise and seemed to have some substance.

Watch your ass, warned Arnold, it could be a veneer.

Yes. All the same, there was something about Nancy that stirred me. The stomach knot that sometimes plagued me when Norman came, came again.

"You're expensive," she said, settling in.

I nodded as I set our glasses of ice water on coasters.

She sniffed. "Those who need help often have no money."

"I sell my energy, not help," I said. "I exchange my energy for money. My fee is what my energy is worth to me."

Nancy did not pursue this.

"I almost didn't come," she said. "Mars is transiting my Venus. That's not a good aspect for new relationships."

I tried to look polite.

Nancy crossed her legs and lit a cigarette. She smiled. "You're a Capricorn, I could tell right away. Capricorns come into their own in later life."

Maybe that's why I don't mind getting older, I thought.

"Of course, I don't believe everything in astrology," said Nancy. "But it often works, you know. Norman and I have studied it for years."

She tugged one ear and licked her lips. "Anyway, here I am." She looked around. "It's a beautiful old house," she said. From where she was sitting you could almost see the swimming pool, but you couldn't miss the oak paneling.

When I first moved here five years ago I was faced with a garden where nothing grew. Overhanging maple and walnut trees blocked almost all the sun. The grass was sick and patchy, flowers did not survive. I decided to give the garden a face-lift. Or, more accurately, Rachel did.

"What you need here," she said, as we sat out taking the shade, "is a swimming pool."

By the next summer it was there. It takes some work to keep it sparkling clean, but it's worth it. If you think of water as a symbol for the unconscious, as I do, there is something very satisfying about having some of it contained in your own back yard—the home of the shadow.

Now, in the heat of summer when others are stuck in traffic jams, driving to and from their weekend cottages, I hole up in my back yard and feel rich.

"Nice plants," remarked Nancy.

They were nothing unusual. Arnold had advised me on what would grow without direct sun: not much.

Nancy got up and inspected my bookcase. She stood a minute and read the framed poem by D.H. Lawrence celebrating elephants:

> The elephant, the huge old beast,
>   is slow to mate;
> he finds a female, they show no haste
>   they wait
>
> for the sympathy in their vast shy hearts
>   slowly, slowly to rouse
> as they loiter along the river-beds
>   and drink and browse
>
> and dash in panic through the brake
>   of forest with the herd,
> and sleep in massive silence, and wake
>   together, without a word.
>
> So slowly the great hot elephant hearts
>   grow full of desire,
> and the great beasts mate in secret at last,
>   hiding their fire.
>
> Oldest they are and the wisest of beasts
>   so they know at last
> how to wait for the loneliest of feasts
>   for the full repast.
>
> They do not snatch, they do not tear;
>   their massive blood
> moves as the moon-tides, near, more near,
>   till they touch in flood.

"He wrote *Lady Chatterley's Lover*," said Nancy, wrinkling her nose. "He had a dirty mind."

I said nothing. She was paying.

"So you like elephants," said Nancy, moving to the mantelpiece where a few dozen guarded my turf. She turned them over and hummed to herself. "Personally I'm partial to cats. I like their independence."

Cats. Yes. There is a great deal of symbolism associated with cats. Some of it I know. A cat proverbially hates dogs and water and is fond of fish. The word cat originally meant stick; this got mixed up in popular usage with broomsticks, hence they are reputed to be familiars of witches. Cats have both solar and lunar characteristics, but the latter predominate. The virgin moon-goddess Artemis-Diana often took the shape of a cat, as did Hecate, the old crone; the Teutonic fertility goddess Freya had a chariot drawn by two cats. They are a ubiquitous symbol of the feminine, known for their free expression of lust and savage love-making.

On the one hand cats are clean and playful and possess oracular powers. On the other, they are associated with female coquetry, the use of their grace for dubious ends.

I've had cats, plenty; they just don't compare with elephants.

Nancy was now looking at the pictures on my walls.

"Ugh!" she said, stopping at a stylized representation of a soaring loon. It was one of my favorites, a signed print by Benjamin Chee Chee, a North American Indian.

"It's so . . . so . . . *pointed,*" said Nancy.

Meanwhile, time was passing. Yes, she was paying, but so was I. This wasn't why she'd come.

"My God, what's *that?*"

Nancy had spotted a piece of sculpture by my old friend Ygor, a bear of a man who lives on an island off British Columbia. It's a glass box with some antique radio tubes and a huge chunk of natural crystal. The outside is decorated with thick black waves. Ygor calls it *Schematic Radio Broadcaster.* It's one of his orphans, so-called because they have no natural homes. It cost me a pretty penny.

Nancy shook her head. I must admit it's a bit strange. At first sight, anyway. But it's nothing compared to Ygor's *Venus of Hornby Island,* made of hundreds of light-bulbs. Over the years I've grown to appreciate his orphans. That's why I keep them in mind for covers of books.

I was not embarrassed at having my taste in art and literature on display, nor did I feel inclined to defend it. It was my choice to practice in my house, in my living room. It's really quite convenient. There is a foyer that doubles as a waiting room. My secretary has an office on the second floor, my daughter lives on the third. And the basement, of course, is full of books.

Not all analysts would be comfortable practicing in their own homes. In fact many counsel against it. They speak of maintaining the frame of analysis.

I understand the frame to mean those aspects of the analytic situation that are more or less controllable by the analyst, such as who sits where, the position of the furniture, what's on the walls, time and place of appointments, opening and closing rituals, etc. It is recommended that the physical setting be impersonal, void of any evidence of the analyst's actual life. The analyst should be unobtrusive, they say; the analysand may then better project unconscious contents onto the analyst.

They have theories and case material to support their view, but I am not persuaded. To my mind it is simply a throw-back to Freudian analysis, where you don't even sit face to face.

I have seen colorless, antiseptic offices intended to be impersonal. I have seen analysts' consulting rooms that are more like lawyers' offices than a haven for the soul. They are certainly not impersonal. The only impersonal setting is a room with no furniture and nothing on the walls. And even that makes a statement about whoever would choose to practice there.

I don't doubt that the frame is significant. Of course, why not? Everything else is. When you're in analysis, it's all grist for the mill. It's like a rotten childhood. If you had one, you work on that; if you didn't, you work on something else.

Jung himself practiced at home. That's enough for me.

Nancy finally exhausted her interest in my decor. She sat down and lit another cigarette. It was now fifteen minutes into the hour.

"I'm really here about Norman," she said.

I waited.

"He writes me," said Nancy, butting out. "But I don't recognize him. I think he's gone off the deep end. What do you think?" She leaned forward. Her perfume was heady. "I mean tell me what you really think."

I was now on my toes. Thank you, Arnold.

"I haven't heard from him lately," I white-lied. After all, it was only a postcard.

Nancy took a piece of paper from her purse.

"Listen to this," she said. " 'Having a terrific time. The weather is fine and the food is great. I miss you and the kids, but not too much. Everything here is very exciting. I am enjoying the change and hope everything's okay with you.'

"That's not like Norman," said Nancy. "I'm sure he's just lost out there."

"I understood that you had separated," I said. "He's on his own now."

Nancy shifted in her chair. "That's just temporary. I know Norman. He'll be back. He can't stay away from home for long without getting anxious."

Norman had told me as much himself. But that was then.

"Maybe he's changed," I said.

Nancy showed a tight smile. It twisted the corners of her mouth and marred her cover.

Marred her cover? said Rachel. Don't you see she's frightened?

In fact, I didn't, not at that point.

"He's conned you," said Nancy.

She stabbed a finger at me. "Listen mister analyst, this man is in trouble. I'm not concerned for myself, but for the kids. 'Why did Daddy leave?' asks Ian. 'When's he coming back?' Jennifer cries herself to sleep. I don't know what to tell them. I was hoping you could talk some sense into him."

There it was, why she came—to get at Norman through me.

I shrugged.

She jumped up and knocked over my precious elephant lamp.

"You don't give a shit!" she shouted. "You don't care about him at all!"

I replaced the lamp while she stormed.

"It's all your doing," she said, pacing the room. "We had a happy family before he started seeing you. It hasn't been easy but God knows I've tried. I've laughed at his dumb jokes, I've entertained his stupid business friends. I've stood by him all the way!"

I reckoned the size of the knot and jumped in.

"You seem to have an expectation of Norman that he's not living up to."

"I love him," she said, defiantly.

I nodded. "I believe you. The question is, who do you love?—Norman as he is, or your image of him?"

That stopped her. But not for long.

"There is no difference," she said firmly.

Tough cookie, said Arnold.

Have a heart, said Rachel, her suffering is as real as Norman's.

I tried another tack.

"How do you feel about your relationship with Norman?" I asked.

Nancy smiled. "Norman and I are very good friends. We've had a good life together. Everyone envies us."

Look out, said Rachel, we've been here before.

"Why do you think he goes with other women?" I asked.

Nancy looked uncomfortable. "I'm sure I don't know. I'm always there, I've never denied him. I'm a good wife. I cook his meals and sleep with him. I iron his shirts and sew his buttons on and raise his children. I think I'm a good mother."

A good mother. What a great thing to have! I had one too. More, I had two, once. My mother and my wife. The first was just fine, the second was not.

"Norman's not even home half the time," said Nancy. "And when he is, he's playing with paints in the basement and getting stoned. Oh yes, I don't know what he told you but he still smokes grass. When he's high he talks of being a hero and slaying dragons, like some kind of Saint George. He used to be a great help to me. Now he doesn't cut the grass and he won't do the dishes. It's not easy to live with, but I try."

I remembered a description of Saint George, in Funk & Wagnall's *Standard Dictionary of Folklore, Mythology and Legend:* "St. George is particularly remembered for his adventures with the dragon (known to every schoolboy) and his prowess in fertilizing barren woman (carefully kept from the youth of England)."

Good luck Norman, I thought.

Nancy was watching me.

"So he has other women. I don't like it but I don't complain. I've never put a hold on Norman. Why should I? He's a grown man, he's free to do what he wants. He always comes home. That's enough for me."

Nancy spoke as if Norman and she were still together. It was quite confusing. I leaned forward. "Norman left you. How do you feel about that? Do you know why?"

She tucked her head in her shoulder and looked sideways. She reminded me of a wounded bird, or Blanche, say, in *Streetcar Named Desire*. She played with her fingers. "Norman just needs some time to himself. He will come back, you'll see."

Now, said Arnold, put it to her.

"Tell me about your father," I said.

Nancy's face slowly crumbled. She started crying.

You bastard, said Rachel.

I passed the kleenex.

"My father was an alcoholic," said Nancy, dabbing her eyes. "He wandered off when I was four years old. I still remember a lot about him. He was a quiet drunk, never violent. He listened to hockey games and played silly games with me. He had no education, he worked his way up to be foreman in a factory. He was always nice to me. I suppose he was a weak man but I know he loved his family. After he left, my mother wouldn't allow him to see us, and finally he stopped trying. I don't know what's become of him."

The absent father motif. A very important factor in the psychological makeup of women whose fathers left or died in the early years. One way or another, these women become fathers' daughters. The early projections onto the father persist into adulthood without the mitigating effect of reality. A woman with an absent father invariably has difficulty relating to men. They can never live up to her expectations.

"I have no one," Nancy was saying. "I'm all alone. I had two older brothers and an aunt. They all died when I was young. My mother passed away three years ago. Everyone I've ever loved has left me. Norman always told me this was forever. And now he's gone too."

She cried softly.

You see how fragile she is, said Rachel.

Yes. Without her fantasy life with Norman, Nancy was defenseless. I regretted sticking in the knife. I'm usually quite gentle. What can I say? Opinionated women drive me crazy. Well, sometimes. Then my ruthless shadow takes over.

An absent father has many and various consequences, depending on specific circumstances. Just as the puer's heroic task is to deal with his mother complex, so the puella has to grapple with her idea of the father.

The absent father is an archetypal motif that can manifest as a feeling of worthlessness and the fear of abandonment. An avowed scorn for men might go hand in hand with a secret admiration. Men may be seen as whimsical and undependable creatures or as just the opposite—faithful and ever true. They may be worshiped as god-like, omnipotent, or ridiculed for their incapacities. And as in everything else psychological, the attitudes up front, out in the open, are unconsciously compensated by their opposites. The animus of the mother, of course, plays a huge role in the father's absence. But that's another story.[1]

I sipped my ice water and looked at the wall. "You have your friend, what's his name . . . Boris?"

Nancy tossed her head. "Boris?! That's a laugh. Boris is no different from Norman. He stopped coming as soon as Norman moved out. You men are all the same—big kids!" she spat. "You can't stand responsibility!"

---

[1] See Marion Woodman, *Addiction to Perfection: The Still Unravished Bride* (Toronto: Inner City Books, 1982) and *The Pregnant Virgin: A Process of Psychological Transformation* (Toronto: Inner City Books, 1985).

I flinched, but stayed in the ring.

"It must be pretty tough, on your own with two small children," I said, patting her hand.

Really! said Rachel.

Nancy pulled away. "Don't patronize me!" she said. "It's all your fault! I've gone without, while Norman spent our money seeing you! And then he left!"

Yes. Money is energy. Norman put his energy into analysis instead of buying vegetables for his family. That was Norman's priority, not mine. I did not blame Nancy for her resentment. Good men are hard to find. Or so I'm told.

We sat in silence. Nancy sniffled. Her persona was completely shot. While Norman was out there finding himself, she was left behind, a lost little girl. After a year of analysis, Norman had a good idea of what he was doing and why. Nancy knew only that she didn't want him to do it.

Norman and Nancy are still pretty close, psychologically. She doesn't see his reality, he can't live up to hers. She is hoping to reestablish their connection, he is trying his damnedest to find something else.

I could not help thinking of Beatrice, my former wife. That's the power of a complex.

My wife and I married young. For a few years we were crazy in love. At least I was. We had a relationship much like that of Norman and Nancy—very close. We were inseparable, we did everything together. Then the rot set in. The details do not much matter. We were unconscious, as most young newlyweds are. The pattern was similar to thousands of other failed marriages. The intention to make them work may be there, but the wherewithal is harder to come by. People do not grow up as easily as they slip a ring on a finger.

Typologically we were well suited, Bea and I. I was introverted—thoughtful, shy and hesitant in groups. She was extraverted—outgoing, adventurous, confident in the world. I took care of reflection, she saw to the initiative and practical action. We relied on each other for what we ourselves didn't have, couldn't do. One was complementary to the other. We fell in love and married because of a psychological predilection for our opposite. It was all very cosy.

Jung himself acknowledged that such relationships are ideal as long as the partners are busy adapting to outside life.

> But when external necessity no longer presses, then they have time to occupy themselves with one another. Hitherto they stood back to back and defended themselves against necessity. But now they turn face to face and look for understanding—only to discover that they have never understood one another.[2]

That's more or less what happened. And the end of our symbiotic union was a severe shock to us both.

Long before we separated, I knew things weren't right between my wife and I. I did nothing about it because we had three children, we were well established as a couple and a family. Most of all, I needed her. I called her Lady in those days. That's a measure of my projection—how I saw her, what I wanted her to be.

Like Norman, I couldn't imagine life without my wife and kids.

One day, hurting inside, while cleaning out the eaves troughs I was stung by a swarm of bees.

Instantly I broke into a sweat. I fell off the ladder. My tongue swelled up. I couldn't speak, I couldn't breathe. An ambulance rushed me to the local hospital. When I woke up the next day a doctor told me I'd had a severe allergic reaction.

I'd never been allergic to anything before. Subsequent tests turned up nothing, but for a long time I carried a vial of adrenalin pills in case it happened again. I didn't understand this incident until it came up in my analysis some years later.

My analyst bobbed his head. "Perhaps it was synchronistic," he said.

"Synchronistic?" I said blankly.

"It's when something happens outside that has a meaning similar to what is going on inside."

It took a few seconds but I made the connection.

---

[2] *Two Essays on Analytical Psychology,* CW 7, par. 80.

"You mean bee—Bea?" I said incredulously.

My analyst shrugged. "It is possible. More than once you've told me you were stung by your wife's attitude."

I found this hard to take in. I was a rational man. I prided myself on living in the real world. I had never joined the Rosicrucians and I had no interest in Ouija boards or psychic healing. Pushed to the wall, I might concede that life is a mystery, but I did not question its meaning. I had studied maths and physics and was quite satisfied with a mechanistic view of the world.

At that time I shared a collective belief in the supremacy of thinking. This is a legacy from the historical period called the Enlightenment or the Age of Reason, roughly the years between 1750 and 1850. Those years marked the transition from life lived according to religious faith, to a reliance on reasoned thinking and what we have come to call scientific thought.

The strength of science is rooted in causal thinking, the principle of cause and effect. Whatever happens is caused by something else. This works both ways: when you know the cause, you can postulate an effect; if you know the effect, you can work back to the cause. It is the common ground of mathematics and engineering, social science, biology and medicine. Cause and effect is the foundation on which modern civilizations have been built. Cold causes water to freeze. Highways buckle in hot weather. Bridges collapse under too much stress.

On the psychological level, this was Freud's way of thinking: a person has a neurosis as a result of a childhood trauma. One's task as an adult is to work on what went awry in the early years.

Causal thinking has traditionally created a separation between psychic events and physical events. Physical causes have effects in the physical world; psychological problems have psychic causes.

More recently there is a growing belief that cause and effect can cross the line, so to speak, that psychic events can have a physical effect and vice versa. Experiments on extrasensory perception suggest this is a distinct possibility, and it is the central question in the area of psychosomatic medicine.

Synchronistic thinking is quite different, but it is not new. The Chinese have practiced it for centuries. They ask, "What likes to happen together in a meaningful way, in the same moment?" It is the basis for the I Ching, the ancient Chinese book of wisdom, Tarot cards, astrology and the oracular reading of animals' entrails. The main difference between synchronistic and causal thinking is the former's focus on time as the central factor.

Jung spoke of synchronicity as meaningful coincidence. We see it at work in the simultaneous occurrence of events, physical or psychic, that are meaningfully related in time but have no rational, cause-and-effect connection.[3]

There was no rational connection between the stinging bees and my inner distress. Nevertheless, they coincided in time. That's synchronicity. Like my chance encounter with a tiny wooden elephant on a path in the Zurich hills. Like anything that happens outside that is relevant to your inner life.

If you notice.

*

We talked awhile longer, Nancy and I, but it was not comfortable. The only thing we shared was the fence between us. Nancy was not interested in looking at herself psychologically. She could not hear what I had to say. The way she saw it, Norman had abandoned his family and would soon realize his mistake. To my mind, he had left under duress. They were both suffering. He was doing something about it, she wasn't.

I grant you, she was left holding a heavier bag.

I helped Nancy on with her coat. In spite of everything I liked her. It took a lot of courage to come to see me.

---

[3] See Jung, "Synchronicity: An Acausal Connecting Principle," *The Structure and Dynamics of the Psyche,* CW 8, and Marie-Louise von Franz, *On Divination and Synchronicity: The Psychology of Meaningful Chance* (Toronto: Inner City Books, 1980).

"Thank you," she said.

I thought of my Zurich analyst's parting remark after a session. *"Auf Wiedersehn,"* he'd say, with a slight smile. "I leave you to your fate."

Perhaps in a few years I'll dare to say as much myself.

"Good-by," I said, taking Nancy's check. "Good luck."

5

Look Homeward, Devil

By whatever means the deep centre is discovered, the great and abiding problem is to hold to it. . . . In the end, the only means by which consciousness can hold to the deep centre is by the continuous discovery and rediscovery that any other way of life has become impossible.
— P.W. Martin, *Experiment in Depth.*

"I missed you," said Norman.

It was our first session since his return from Europe. He was very excited. I was glad to see him.

"It was just great!" he said. "I wanted to tell you everything."

I knew the feeling. What happens isn't real until you share it with someone close.

I smiled. "You enjoyed yourself?"

"That's too mild," said Norman.

I would not venture more.

"It would be truer to say I *was* myself," said Norman.

My imagination took off, but I said nothing.

"I landed in Paris at ten in the p.m.," said Norman. "The airport was chaos. There had just been a terrorist attack in Beirut and the security was tighter than screw. People were everywhere, speaking languages I didn't recognize. I grabbed my suitcase off a conveyor belt and hailed a cab.

"To the Seine!" I cried.

" *'Comment?'* said the cabbie.

"Well, my accent isn't so good, but we got there. I strolled along the river bank and my heart was full. For the first time in years I felt free. I had no cares. For a moment I thought of Nancy and the kids, then they disappeared. I was alone by the water, alone in Paris!"

Norman leaned forward. "Do you know what that's like?"

I would not upstage him.

"Tell me," I said.

"I'd read about Paris," said Norman, "I'd seen the pictures. I'd talked to people who'd been there. But nothing prepared me for the actual experience, the glorious reality, of walking along the Seine. It was absolutely magical!"

"Yes," I nodded.

"I left the river and strolled along Boulevard St. Germaine. The Left Bank! God, I couldn't believe it! I watched wizened old men and laughing girls try their luck at roulette-wheel booths. I played pin-ball machines on the rue Buci. I had a beer in the Café Monaco. At a sidewalk stall I bought a Degas print and some books."

Norman fished in his briefcase.

"Here," he said, "I brought you a present."

He handed me a copy of Henry Miller's *Black Spring*. A first edition, very rare.

"Thank you," I said, turning it over. I was moved.

"In the Deux Maggots I had a glass of cold white wine," said Norman. "I watched the parade and eyed-balled pretty girls. They passed me by, but they smiled. I moved on to the Café Flores where I was propositioned by an Algerian student and a French businessman. I turned them down, cheerfully."

Norman gathered his thoughts.

"I hauled my bag to the Hotel du Hâvre, a pension I'd read about. Fifty francs a night, very cheap. The concierge spoke no English, she thought I was a Dane.

" *'Faites comme vous voulez,'* she said, bowing.

"I understood this to mean I could do whatever I wanted. The room was clean and mirrored on all sides, even the ceiling! There were two chairs and a table, and a bidet tucked behind a curtain. I fell asleep beside myself. There was nowhere I'd rather be.

"The next day I went to the Louvre and spent a couple of hours getting lost. I saw the Mona Lisa. I saw Utrillo, van Gogh and Chagall. Thrilling! I wandered through rooms of Greek and Roman sculpture. I walked round and round the heads of Adonis and Eros and Hermes. I'd read they come to life when you're in motion. They did, I was ecstatic. It was a great day, I saw a lot."

Norman looked at his hands.

"By five o'clock I was lonely. I wished you were there. I wished Nancy was there. I wanted my kids."

I could picture it well enough. The same thing hit me the first Christmas in Zurich. I desperately missed my family. It was almost more than I could stand.

"Dammit, Arnold," I said aloud, "help me through the night with one of your parties."

But Arnold wasn't there. He'd finagled his way back to Canada to be with loved ones. I felt deserted. I knew of others who were alone, who would welcome a get-together, but without Arnold I could not muster the energy.

My analyst had no patience with poor me. I saw him on Christmas Eve when, had the gods been willing, I would have been Home, opening presents under the tree.

"You're whining in the manger," he said. "Christmas is a time for new life, not for dying. Save that for Easter."

Norman blew his nose and continued.

"I went to the Foyer des Etudiants, behind the Pantheon. Nobody questioned me so I got in to eat. I watched the students chatter and wished I were one of them. A girl across the table looked at me with some interest, I thought, but just as I was leaning over to make contact a young punk in a motorcycle jacket took her away.

"I recovered somewhat at the opera. Who can stay depressed in that setting? I had a rush seat in the fourth balcony, a panoramic view. They say it's where the gods sit, marking time. There was a chandelier fit for a railway station. I watched it sway and listened to the voices. It was *Rigoletto,* in Italian. I didn't understand a word but I cried for two hours.

"Sitting beside me was Ronald, a one-eyed black man from Nairobi. He was a pleasant chap. He bought me cognacs in the intervals. He pressed my arm as we left.

" 'You like to come home with me, this very night?' said Ronald, flashing teeth.

" So help me, I almost said yes.

"The lonely had snuck back in. With a heavy heart I started back to my pension. It was a long haul. I went by way of the Bastille because it was a landmark. I thought of all those poor buggers killed storming it. What for? Life hasn't changed. You still get offered cake when all you want is bread.

"I stopped on the Ile de St. Louis and watched a group of students, half a dozen, mixing French street songs with rock and roll. They danced as they sang, arm in arm. Oh joy, oh simple delight! I was overwhelmed. The tears rolled.

"I was about to move on when one of the young men came over and plucked my sleeve.

" 'Oh! *mon cher,* you are sad!' " he said. 'Come, join us!'

"I danced with them and we drank some wine. They were cheerful and gay. It was exhilarating. We caught our breath in a café, where we drank Pernod with an evil mixture of white wine and blackberry liqueur called *blanc cassis.*

"My spirits soared. We chatted away like old friends. They knew some English, I struggled along in French. Then they took me to Les Halles, the Paris market."

Norman flung his arms out.

"Well! You've not seen anything like that! It was four o'clock in the morning but in the market it was like noon: hawkers everywhere, vegetable stalls, fruit sellers, meat mongers toting huge sides of beef. The noise! The smells! The feel of the place! Ladies of the night hung around the corners, reaching out. We skipped along the aisles, copping loose fruit.

"By then I had fallen in love with Monique, one of the students. She was cute as a button. She looked like a little girl, but she said she was twenty-five. Monique was studying Russian literature. She looked at me as if I were the only man on earth. I floated through the market, her arm in mine, and thought ain't life grand.

"As dawn was breaking, we split up.

"Monique pressed her lips to my ear. *'Cherie,'* she whispered, 'I want to be with you.'

"I was nothing loathe. We trotted across the Seine to my pension. The concierge was very polite. 'The mademoiselle must register for the police, messieur. *C'est normale.*"

"Monique signed in. Then we were alone in the elevator, going up. She smiled at me, an open smile, at ease. She hugged me, fingers light on my spine. She brushed my cheek with her eyelashes and, well, she *cooed.*

"You know what?" said Norman. "I thought of your Mr. Appleby and mice in the cake mix! If you can't let go, you can't take off, right?"

I smiled. Now how did he know about Mr. Appleby?

"Monique undressed slowly," said Norman, "not demure or shy. Not coy or affected or embarrassed. She faired her toilette in the bidet. She took off her glasses and turned to face me. Little girl indeed! My heart jumped for joy, like a schoolboy. She hopped into bed and slid between the sheets. Trembling, I joined her. She pressed against me, hungry, full of life."

Norman looked into space.

"What can I say? The rising sun filled the room. Sounds of Paris floated in the window. Outside were lonely men and women. People were in prison, marooned on islands, locked in the chill embrace of the workaday world. Why, the stock market fell fifteen points that very day.

"I reveled in the moment. Monique's hair, long and soft, brushed my chest. I stroked her cheeks, watching us in the mirror opposite. Her eyes were closed, her breath came quick and even, lips moistly parted, receiving the host. I listened to the lapping of my tide. It was delicious.

"So this is Paris, I thought. People are starving. Many have no homes. They sleep on subway gratings for the rising heat. I gave them a fleeting thought and felt blessed.

"It was an interesting time. Monique showed me some things that maybe only French women know. I was grateful for that. We finally fell asleep, exhausted. I woke up about noon. Monique was gone, and so was my wallet."

Norman clapped his hands and laughed.

"Shit, I didn't even care! There wasn't much money in it, and my credit cards were with my passport. I figured it was a damn small price to pay."

He took out his notebook.

"The rest of the time wasn't so dramatic, but there were moments. I didn't feel lonely after that. Sure I had a few bleak spots, but there was always something new. I went back to the opera and got to know what was happening. I saw some ballet and a few plays. I went through umpteen museums. I hung out in bars and talked to people.

"My favorite place was Kelly's, a bar near the American Express office. The waitresses were polite, they laughed at my simple jokes in French and asked for more. Sometimes I took a sketch pad and drew portraits of the other customers."

Norman grinned. "The drawings weren't very good. The spin-off, however, was considerable."

I listened with nostalgia. It was a typical puer gambit. I'd done much the same in Zurich. Could he read my mind?

"Time went quickly, I was never at a loss," said Norman. "The weather was fine, I walked a lot. I sat on a bench in the Bois de Boulogne and watched the children play. People sat beside me and talked about themselves. I fed the swans and felt good.

"It was a new experience for me, having nothing to do. I became philosophical. At night I looked at the stars and reflected on my life, where I was and what I'd been. I thought about how it used to be with Nancy."

Here it comes, said Rachel. Get out the kleenex, said Arnold.

"Tell me," I said.

"The first years were wonderful," said Norman. "We had fun together, I enjoyed being a family man.

"One summer we swapped houses with a couple who lived in a rural village. They had an old farmhouse with low doorways and beamed ceilings. It was really Nancy's idea, she loves the country. She was carrying Jennifer then and said the fresh air would do her good.

"I can see her now, sitting on a window seat, smiling. She was reading a seed catalogue.

" 'Do you want to know what ants do?'

" 'Eh?' I was playing on the floor with Ian, building a rocket launcher with Lego.

" 'Ants,' " said Nancy. "She read from the catalogue: 'Ants steal seeds but do no injury to growing plants. However, they loosen the soil around the roots so that plants wilt and die. Ants also carry greenfly from one plant to another, and anthills disfigure the lawn.'

" 'I knew all that.'

"Nancy sniffed. 'You can't tell a daffodil from a tulip.'

" 'That isn't true. Daffodils are yellow.'

"Just down the road from us was an old church. There was a notice on the door:

> This is NOT a children's playground. Boys and girls found running about the church in a rowdy manner will be dismissed and reported to the police.

"I penciled under this: 'Suffer little children . . .' I don't remember why. As a father I'm pretty Victorian myself.

"The village hall was also the schoolhouse. The Women's Institute used it for amateur plays, jumble sales and dances. It was the local library on Tuesdays and Thursdays between 7 and 9 p.m. and the doctor's office on Wednesdays at noon.

"We went to some of the dances. They were called loo dances because they were saving up to put in a toilet. There was cold beer, a piano and a man who played the fiddle. It was square dancing, Virginia reels and do-see-do. Nancy had too much to drink and got giggly. At 10.30 there were sandwiches and a draw for the door prize. Nancy won a pair of stockings once. There was a chemical toilet for the ladies and the men went outside."

Norman grinned.

"Can you imagine this place? The corner store had a cracker barrel! There was a village green where they still played cricket! When men passed you in the street they tipped their hats! And the ladies nodded! It was like living in another century."

I had some questions, but you don't stop someone on a roll.

"The vicar came to call one day. Nancy got in a flap when she saw him coming up the walk.

" 'Quick!' she cried. 'Put your suit on!'

"I was half way up the stairs when I realized all my suits were at the cleaners. Nancy rushed around shoving toys behind the sofa. She gathered up piles of laundry and ran toward the basement. She hit her head going through the door and fell down.

"At that moment Ian, who'd been eating soap flakes in the bathroom, slipped and started screaming. Nancy lay crying on the floor as the vicar knocked.

"I rescued Ian while Nancy crawled to the kitchen and out the back. I gathered she didn't want to meet anybody. Ian squirmed. Holding him by one foot I opened the front door and greeted the vicar.

" 'Mr. Jolly!' I said heartily. I knew his name because just that morning we'd received the church newsletter. It began, 'The motorcar has come to our village, with a vengeance! What would our forebears have said?'

"We shook hands for a few minutes. I cleared an armchair for him to sit on. Ian was quiet but he was turning purple. I turned him over and gave him a healthy belt.

"Pardon me," I said to the vicar. ""It helps the colic."

Ian coughed and smiled at me. I propped him up in a corner with a stuffed unicorn.

"Mr. Jolly was elfin. His head was tiny, his body was thin, he had little pointed ears. His feet didn't quite reach the floor. He had a bright smile. He folded his hands and looked around with interest.

" 'There's history here,' he said, smiling, dangling his feet.

" 'There is?'

" 'I can feel it,' said Mr. Jolly. 'It's in the walls.'

"I had one eye on Ian, threading his way through the laundry. He reached me dragging a brassiere and started climbing up my pants. I shook my leg but he kept coming. I asked Mr. Jolly if he'd mind holding Ian while I made a pot of tea.

" 'My wife's in bed,' I explained. 'She has chicken pox.'

"In the kitchen I filled the kettle. There was a tapping on the back window. This took me by surprise as the only window in the kitchen was a skylight over the sink. I looked up. Nancy was holding her head and making faces. I made motions to mean she was sleeping and she shook her fist. I blew her a kiss and made the tea.

"Back in the living room Ian was exploring the vicar's nose. He had come through his diapers and there were little trickles of wet on Mr. Jolly's trousers. Ian's lower lip was flat out. That meant he was about to cry.

" 'I'm so sorry,' I said, 'I'd better change him.'

"Mr. Jolly said he loved little children, they were the real people. I left him staring down at a coffee table with a Formica top; embedded in it were advertisements from an old veterinary journal.

Teat slitter, with concealed blade and finger rings, nickle-plated. 75¢

Castrating clamp for sheep, pigs, etc., with ratchet closure, bright finish, in leatherette pouch. $1.50

Balling gun, Fook's, for horse balls, with rubber mouthpiece. $1.95

"We had tea in some mugs Nancy made. The handles were crooked but I couldn't find anything else. Mr. Jolly asked me what line of business I was in.

" 'Food,' I said. "I wholesale to the chains."

"Mr Jolly nodded and bit into a cinnamon bun. He wiped his lips with a napkin and said, 'How do you find these parts?'

" 'It's just beautiful around here.'

"He nodded. 'Surely, God's own country.'

"He asked if my good lady enjoyed the village life. I told him she'd like to live there all the time, we were thinking of buying a place of our own. That was true.

"Mr. Jolly crossed his legs. 'I grow my own tobacco,' he said.

"I thought about my marijuana plants and laughed. 'I'm trying to give up smoking,' I said. That wasn't true.

"We sipped our tea in silence. An old grandfather clock ticked. We watched Ian suck on a toothpaste tube.

"Dear, precious Ian, our first-born, the apple of our eye. For the first few months we called him Cricket because he lay in his cot with his legs in the air and rubbed his feet together. After he'd rocked two cribs to pieces we called him Brutus. And when he started a bonfire with my sales reports I called him Justified—I felt guilty for being away so much."

I was reminded of the habit I used to have of renaming people—giving them nicknames. It's very common, of course. I thought nothing of it until a close friend I'd blithely called Orange for years—his last name was Peel—told me how much he resented it.

"It proscribes my identity," he said. "I feel trapped. It denies me the freedom to be myself."

He was right. Renaming, nicknaming, is a magical procedure. Whether it's Earl the Pearl, Lady, Louie the Lip or Waterfall Eagle, the aim is to assign the other person an identity you can cope with. It has its roots in projection and carries with it certain expectations. Of course, the person who identifies with a nickname, and therefore feels inhibited by it—like my friend Orange—has a problem too, but that's something else.

What about Honeybunch and Loverboy? asked Rachel. Those too, I replied, and every other loving monicker like Sweetheart, Darling and Princess. All in all, it's pretty harmless. Just something to keep in mind when Dear Heart turns out to be a con man or My Love runs off with your best friend.

Meanwhile, Norman was wallowing in the past.

"There was scrambled egg on Ian's face that wouldn't come off. And snot, always the snot. You could scrub all day and it would still be there. I took away the toothpaste and gave him a cream cracker. He munched on it, talking to his toes.

"Mr. Jolly tickled Ian's chin and made some noises in his throat.

"After awhile it began to get dark. Mr. Jolly sighed and wriggled off the chair. 'I'll be going now,' he said, 'there's Evensong soon.'

" 'Glad you dropped in.'

" 'Tell your good lady I hope she gets well.'

" 'She'll be sorry she missed you.'

" 'I'll come again.'

" 'Please do, anytime.'

"I waved him down the walk and closed the door. Nancy came running in, all smiles. She threw her arms around me. 'I heard it all,' she said, 'you were wonderful!'

There were now tears in Norman's eyes.

"We were happy in the country, maybe we should have bought a house there."

I passed the kleenex.

He blew his nose.

We'd been here before, Norman and I. Whenever he thought of his family, he became sentimental. Sentimentality is a sure sign of an activated mother complex. Feelings that were once appropriate, a natural expression of the life force, come back to haunt you. That's what regression looks like.

Norman had had some dreams during his time in Paris. He had mulled them over and made detailed notes. They told us little we didn't already know. He longed for the irretrievable past, while the future hadn't yet grabbed him.

It was near the end of the hour when Norman put his notebook down and said: "I hear you saw Nancy."

I felt a stab of guilt.

"I gave nothing away," I said.

Norman tossed his head. "I was really pissed off when she told me. Now why would he do that, I thought."

I squirmed.

"Simple, you couldn't say no, right?!"

I nodded weakly.

"Never mind," he said, "she's a witch. I came back feeling terrific. The kids were glad to see me, they jumped up and down and hugged me. Nancy stood off to one side looking resentful.

"I'd brought her a lovely silk shawl from Paris. 'It's very fashionable,' I said. 'You see them everywhere.'

"She hardly looked at it.

"I watched myself. You know what? In half an hour I was feeling awful! I had back spasms and a headache. My stomach was in knots. What can I do, I thought, to make her feel better?"

Norman paced the room.

"I saw it, plain as day. In Nancy's presence I can barely function. It's hard to believe but it's true. I don't know what to say. I whine and get defensive. I want to throw myself on the floor and beg forgiveness. For what? I don't know.

"All evening she complained about her life.

" 'It's no picnic with two kids and no man around the house,' she said pointedly.

"I shrunk.

" 'I never wanted a life like this,' she said.

"I winced.

" 'I could have married into wealth,' she said.

"I cringed.

"When it was time to go to bed I tried a playful squeeze but she pulled away. She called me a selfish chauvinist and said I could sleep in the guest room. There weren't even any pillows!"

Norman wrung his hands. "Maybe she's right, I ask too much."

Laugh or cry, it was clear to me that Norman's survival was at stake. In my mind that was easily distinguished from selfishness. He'd been ambushed, yet again, by his own psychology. I wasn't comfortable taking sides, but what can you do. Norman was no good to Nancy or himself the way he was. I jumped in with both feet.

"There is a grave danger," I said, "that unless you hang on to where you got to, you will fall back to where you were—and perhaps even further."

Norman was taken aback.

I plunged on.

"I don't believe it's chauvinistic to want to live with a woman who's sexually interested in you. That's a fact of human nature, an archetypal mode of functioning. It's an indication of your wife's power over you that she could make you question something so obvious. I'm amazed she can so easily persuade you that your natural feelings are wrong."

Norman pursed his lips and frowned.

"Your wife wants men friends and no questions asked. The very idea hurts but you think you ought to be able to stand it. So you agree with her and then you feel worse! Well, I'm not surprised. You're trying to talk yourself into something that goes against the grain. Meanwhile, you have fundamental and legitimate needs that aren't being met."

Norman hung his head.

"To be happy with your wife you would need her help in establishing a different feeling atmosphere between you. I'd be very surprised if you got it. Her aim, it seems to me, is to hold on to you in the castrated role of very best friend."

Norman blew his nose and stared at the floor.

"It doesn't surprise me that you can't bear her suffering. It's the age-old technique by which the mother hangs on to her sons. When we demand our rights as men, she goes all hurt and tragic. 'After all I've done for you!' she cries. Guilty, weighed down with a sense of harsh ingratitude, we slink back into line."

"We?" said Norman, looking up.

Do it, said Rachel, give.

I nodded. "I too have been ravaged by the mother. Few men haven't."

Norman straightened his tie. I saw relief in his eyes, a new light.

He shook my hand at the door. "Thank you," he said, "I needed that."

So did I, I thought, waving him out.

6

Mirror, Mirror, Tell Me True

"I feel like a fly on the wall," said Rachel, "watching it all happen."

I was not displeased.

"You took sides," she said. "Why?"

"I was impatient," I said.

"You're supposed to be objective," Rachel remarked.

"Yes. Well, it isn't always possible. Sometimes I get carried away. I'm not proud of that but it happens. Jung himself said good advice isn't dangerous because it has so little effect. I say a lot of things in an hour. Some of it sinks in, some doesn't. Norman only remembers what is relevant to where he's at."

Rachel thought. It's not her best function.

"Now I'm confused," she said. "Does he really have to leave Nancy—forever?"

"I don't know. Clearly he'd rather not. I know they must separate psychologically, break the bind they're in."

"I'd have thought Norman would see that himself by now," remarked Rachel.

"Oh, he does," I said. "He understands it very well. In his head. But he still gets hooked when he's around his wife. Indeed, so do I. That's the power of the complex."

"So if Norman stopped identifying with Nancy," said Rachel, "could he accept her as she is and make the best of it?"

"That's a good question," I said.

"And if he could manage that, could his wife accept what he'd become any more than she can accept him as he is now?"

"That's another," I agreed.

We sat a moment in silence. These were enormous questions. I had no answers.

"In any case," I said, "A lot of Norman's energy is still invested in his relationship with Nancy. You watch, the complex tells him they still have a chance."

"My God," said Rachel, "he's back and forth like a yo-yo! I want to wring his neck. How do you stand it?"

I shrugged. "Norman is trying. You can't fault a man for what he is. Well, I can't. I can tell him what I see, but not what to do about it. He has to live with the consequences of his actions, I don't."

Rachel mused.

"Where is Norman now?"

"He's finding his feet," I said. "To some extent he's disengaged from the quagmire of his life but he doesn't know where he stands. He's experimenting with possibilities."

"Quagmire," repeated Rachel. "Isn't that rather strong? It's an odd word for his life with Nancy. He enjoyed being a family man."

"I'm glad you brought that up," I said.

Rachel beamed.

"Norman was leading an unexamined life. Was it worth living? Can we even call it happy? When he first came to see me, he was at the end of his rope. Oh yes, he had a wonderful life, he said—but there he was, depressed and anxious. He had no energy, he couldn't stop crying. His life was all persona, a charming mask. He had everything he wanted, but there was nothing about him he could call his own.

"Norman came to me on his knees. What reduced him to tears? He thought it was his wife's infidelity, but that was only the last straw; it precipitated a crisis that deep in Norman was already underway. He had lived on the surface for so long, he had no idea what was going on underneath. His image of himself was false. He did not know who he was.

"However you describe the outer trappings of Norman's life, he was not satisfied. Some of his dissatisfaction stemmed from ignorance of his own psychology. Now he knows rather more about himself than he used to, but he's not out of the woods yet. He resists the next step."

"What's that?" asked Rachel.

"I don't know. But if he wants a different life, one more in tune with who he is, he has to change. He's on the hero's journey, but he still has a life-line to his wife.

"It's like the Russian fairy tale, 'The Virgin Czar,' where the Baba Yaga witch asks the hero, 'My child, are you going voluntarily or involuntarily?' You could spend hours trying to answer that. It's a trick of the mother complex—to raise a philosophical question when action is required.[1] The hero's appropriate response is, 'Shut up and help me pack!' That puts the witch in her place."

"Should Norman say that to Nancy?" asked Rachel.

I laughed.

"God forbid! That would only make a bad situation worse. The wise man says that *to himself.* It helps to depotentiate the complex.

"Nancy has a powerful animus but she's no Baba-Yaga. To Norman she sometimes seems like a witch—a negative mother— because what she says or does constellates that aspect of himself. The hero's real task is to learn how to tell the difference between what's out there and what's in him. Deal with your complexes and the outside world takes on a different light."

I sat back. "Norman is stumbling, but he's on the way. There's an inner imperative at work in him. We don't know where it will lead."

"But you're in charge," said Rachel.

"It may seem that way," I agreed.

"You're writing it," she pressed.

"I'm recording it," I said. "There is a difference."

---

[1] See Marie-Louise von Franz, *Puer Aeternus: A Psychological Study of the Adult Struggle with the Paradise of Childhood,* 2nd ed. (Boston: Sigo Press, 1984), pp. 173ff.

7

The Worm Turns

The united personality will never quite lose the painful sense of innate discord. Complete redemption from the sufferings of this world is and must remain an illusion.
—C.G. Jung, "The Psychology of the Transference."

Be yourself. No one else will.
—Will Rogers, American Folk Hero.

Norman came in looking quite smug. He circled the room like a Spitfire coming in to land. Vroom! Vroom! Here I come!

He just grinned, the sound effects were in my head.

Something's up, I thought. It makes a change, smiled Rachel.

Norman tucked in his landing gear and sat down.

"I want to be an analyst," he said.

I nodded. Almost everyone in analysis has the same thought at some point.

"It hit me like a ton of bricks!" said Norman. "I'm not happy with my life, my job has become meaningless. Why not change course? Why shouldn't I do what you do?"

"Give me a minute," I said. "I'm thinking."

Norman's questions were fair enough. I did not begrudge them. He was as ready to train as I was when I went to Zurich. But why would he? What was his motivation? Did the desire to train spring strictly from the transference—wanting to be like me? Or was it a genuine direction for Norman? Maybe he thought it would be glamorous, being an analyst. Maybe he actually wanted to *help* people.

"Tell me about it," I said.

"Well, it happened like this. I was at a party the other night and got into a conversation with a girl—a woman, I should say. She's a therapist, her name is Nicole. She was born in Uruguay and grew up in Quebec City. She's a great dancer. She told me about her practice and talked about what it felt like. I've never met anyone like her. I was fascinated.

"We ended up back at my place. She looked around at all my drawings on the walls.

" 'It's very comfortable here,' she said, 'it's part of you.'

"I liked that. She didn't think I was crazy.

"We made love at our leisure, as if we had all the time in the world. Have you ever heard of the butterfly waltz? The mulingi shuffle? Nicole has, she says they come from some Eastern tradition. She's into all those New Age things, like vision quests and crystals, past lives and healing stones."

Norman described the butterfly waltz and the mulingi shuffle in colorful detail. Personally, I haven't exhausted the possibilities of the missionary position.

"It was dawn when Nicole left. She wrapped a cloak around her shoulders and kissed me at the door. 'You're a very special man,' she said."

Norman beamed.

I smiled back. I shared his pleasure at finding someone who appreciated him.

I said: "So where are we? What does all that have to do with being an analyst?"

"It hadn't occurred to me before," said Norman. "But the idea caught me. It's like I've been casting around for something to do with my life. This may be it. Meeting Nicole could be synchronistic, don't you think?"

I shrugged. I thought of all the parties in the city, and all the therapists and all the Norman's who might run into each other at one of them. It seemed to me more a question of statistical probability than synchronicity.

On the other hand, I failed statistics at university.

I was of two minds. I could easily prick Norman's balloon. Or I could support him and see what happened next. Would he take some action to make the idea real? I had no strong feeling one way or the other. Certainly I did not know what he should do. That's why I'm an analyst and not a fortune teller.

I chose a middle path, which is to say noncommittal. I would not come down one way or the other, even to myself, without hearing from the unconscious. I had an opinion, that's true, but it would have been foolish to express it. Norman might have substituted it for his own inner imperative.

You took sides before, said Rachel. That was another hour, I said, today's today. Oh, said Rachel.

"Did you dream that night?" I asked.

"No," said Norman. "As a matter of fact I didn't sleep at all. After Nicole left I sipped cognac and watched the sun rise."

"And that day?"

"I called the office and told them I was seeing clients. Then I went for a long walk along the waterfront. It was rush hour, people everywhere. Materialism, advertising, pollution! Everybody hurrying somewhere. A bunch of bloody sheep! It made me sick to think I was one of them."

That kind of remark is a dead giveaway. It goes with the feeling of being special, of having a unique destiny. When you feel like that, it's hard to muster the energy to earn a living. Compared to what you're cut out for, the daily grind is just too mundane. It's a variety of inflation. You feel special. So why, you ask yourself, am I doing something so ordinary?

If this attitude persists, you can cheerfully rationalize wasting your life, waiting for destiny to catch up—or fall from the sky. You play the lotteries. You know the odds are against you but you hope you'll win. You put money into stocks and bonds and you hedge your bets with silver futures.

Meanwhile, life goes on.

Jung makes the following comments on inflation:

> An inflated consciousness is always egocentric and conscious of nothing but its own existence. It is incapable of learning from the past, incapable of understanding contemporary events, and incapable

of drawing right conclusions about the future. It is hypnotized by itself and therefore cannot be argued with. It inevitably dooms itself to calamities that must strike it dead.[1]

Norman was not like that all the time. He just had spells when he forgot he was human. Then the mountain gave him a spill.

I'm no different. Nor is Arnold. He talked to me the other day about death. He hates getting old.

"What did you expect," I said, "eternal youth?"

"There have been times," admitted Arnold, "when I thought I would never die."

Spoken like a true puer. Lapsed, mind you, but all the same.

I turned back to Norman, swimming upstream at rush hour.

"And then?" I asked.

"I went home and slept for a few hours," said Norman.

"And dreamed?"

Norman blushed. "Yes, I did."

He opened his notebook and read: "I'm in a room. There's shit everywhere. I'm slipping and sliding in it. Then I'm on a balcony high above the street. Like a telescope, my eye zooms in on a school of fish wriggling through a stream of traffic. The fish scales sparkle in the sun."

Norman looked up. "It was a weird dream. I don't know what to make of it. Do you?"

It was late afternoon, rainbow time. They danced on the walls, painted the plants. I watched them and thought of fish.

As a teenager, I used to go fishing in the hills of Nova Scotia, tramping the creeks and streams, bringing home ten- and twelve-inch brook trout for my mother to cook. I didn't know then that fish in dreams symbolize contents of the unconscious. They were fun to catch and good to eat. That was enough for me. When the fish were jumpin', so was I.

---

[1] *Psychology and Alchemy,* CW 12, par. 563.

When I was training in Zurich I did a paper on fish. Here are some things I learned:

The yang-yin (male-female) polarity is symbolized in Chinese philosophy as two fish: a black one with a white eye, a white one with a black eye. Together, in a round, they stand for wholeness.

The fisher king in the Grail legend is sick in body and soul until redeemed by the hero who asks the right question.

In alchemy the fish is a symbol of both the *prima materia,* the beginning, and the *lapis,* the highest goal, of the seven-stage process leading to transformation.

In the Talmud the Messiah is called Dag (fish); his second coming is to be in the conjunction of Saturn and Jupiter in Pisces, astrological sign of the two fishes.

A fish's penis is much smaller than an elephant's.

A man's anima, his soul, commonly appears in dreams as a mermaid, a woman with a fish tail, indicating her close connection with the sea of the unconscious.

Fish turn up in many fairy tales as bringers of gifts and helpers in the search for treasure (as in Grimm's "The Sea-Hare").

Jung had a lot to say about fish, particularly as a symbol of Christ, himself a symbol of the Self.[2] In that context the fish stands for redemption through bodily suffering. Elsewhere he wrote:

> The fish in dreams occasionally signifies the unborn child, because the child before its birth lives in the water like a fish; similarly, when the sun sinks into the seas, it becomes child and fish at once. The fish is therefore a symbol of renewal and rebirth.[3]

With some of this in mind I was not at sea with Norman's dream. He's above the hurly-burly of everyday life. He sees possibilities but they aren't yet clear. And he's still in shit, which means there are shadow things to be worked on. The fish scales sparkling in the sun suggest the potential for becoming conscious.

---

[2] *Aion, CW 9ii.*
[3] *Symbols of Transformation,* CW 5, par. 290.

I thought of a remark by Jung—that it makes little difference whether the analyst understands or not; the important thing is that the other person understands what is at work in him.

In terms of dreams, for instance, there is always the danger that the analyst will step in with a preconceived opinion. It may be right, but such a truth reaches only the head. Understanding in analysis aims more at the heart; it is only worthwhile if it comes as an agreement, the fruit of joint reflection. Anything else falls into the category of suggestion, a kind of magic that works in the dark and makes no ethical demands.[4]

"It's a mystery to me," I said. "Go home. Think fish. Read about them. Draw them. Eat them. Go out and try to catch a few. See what gets hooked."

I took my glasses off and set them on the table between us. That's a signal that the hour is over.

Norman gathered his things together. "What about training?" he said. "I've written to Zurich for information."

I was emptying the remains of our glasses into the plants. It saves watering them at the end of the day.

"It's a possibility," I conceded. "Let's see what happens."

*

Alone that night, I got out the Scotch and went back twenty years to when I first thought of training.

I was in analysis in London at the time. I was there because I hurt. My wife and kids were back in Canada, wondering if they'd ever see me again. I didn't know what would happen next. I had a part-time job as a salesman in the jewelry department of Harrod's, purveyor to the Queen. The pay was not good, but there were some perks. They gave you twenty percent off in the meat department and there was a lunchroom on the roof where you got to chat up birds. I was living

---

[4] "The Practical Use of Dream-Analysis," *The Practice of Psychotherapy,* CW 16, par. 303.

in a small flat around the corner, on Onslow Square. I'd been there about six months, eating my heart out.

One weekend, as I arrived at the home of friends in the country, a man was just leaving. He was tall and perhaps fifteen years older than me. He was from London's East End. We had about five minutes together. It was enough. In that time I learned he was training to be a lay analyst.

"A lay analyst?" I asked.

"It means I'm not a medical doctor," he said.

For twenty-five years he had been a shoemaker, of all things. Well, he did own the factory. Now he was just finishing a five-year course at the Sigmund Freud Institute in London.

It struck a chord in me and I plied him with questions.

"I'd rather not talk about it," he smiled. "I'm on vacation."

That impressed me—he knew where he stood.

I did not think of emulating this man. I was not interested in Freud's view of the psyche, nor did I relish lying on a couch four or five times a week, talking to the ceiling. Still, this chance meeting brought to a focus some thoughts I'd been having; namely, what would become of me?

If this man, at his age, could become an analyst, why couldn't I?

I suddenly realized that I was not stuck with life as it was. Anything was possible. That's when Arnold entered my life, not actually but in effect.

It seemed the right thing to do, to train, a natural progression of my own analysis. It was the most challenging thing I could think of, the most demanding, the most rewarding. I got excited thinking about it. Selling jewelry was pretty boring, even in Harrod's. I never got to see the Queen anyway. She didn't shop in person.

And yes, like Norman, I thought the meeting was synchronistic.

I discussed it with Chester, who'd saved my life the day I woke up crying from a dream. He'd referred me to the analyst I was working with. He also got me the job at Harrod's.

I loved Chester. He was an expatriate Canadian with a thriving antique business. He'd gone to London in the early fifties with holes in his pockets. He started out selling trinkets and old books off a barrow in Portobello Road. Then he cornered the market in Impressionist prints and rare china. Now he had a swanky showroom of period furniture in Harrod's and was worth a mint.

We stood elbow to elbow in Finch's, our old haunt on the Fulham Road, trading dreams. Finches had a new guv'nor but the clientele hadn't changed. It still felt good. It was in Finches that I met Chester in the first place—and Ygor too—many years ago, fresh off the monkey plane.

Chester was in the midst of his own midlife crisis. He was then in analysis with the legendary E.A. Bennet, one of the original analysts in England who'd worked with Jung. Like Arnold, Chester's intuition works overtime. That's how he knew what I needed, and who to recommend, when I hollered for help.

Chester was very successful in what he did. That very day he'd sold a whole room of Louis Quinze furniture to a newspaper tycoon. He had a warehouse full of similar stuff and he was negotiating with an Arab to buy the lot.

But Chester wasn't happy. He was having second thoughts about the antique business.

"Sure, there's money in it," he said. "It's a good living, but what for? What does it mean?"

Chester thumped his pint on the bar. "There's more to life than making money, there must be! How much can you eat? How many cars do you need?"

Jostled by the crowd, I lost sight of Chester. That was one of the things about Finches, you never felt lonely. You went with the flow, you talked with strangers. You didn't think about tomorrow. Or, indeed, today.

Crushed in a corner, I rolled a cigarette. I felt a jab in my side. I looked down and saw a midget smiling up at me.

"Can you teach me how to do that with one hand?" he asked.

"I don't know," I said, thinking of John Wayne and other cowpokes. I had no personal need to roll cigarettes with one hand, but maybe he was a jockey.

"What about two?"

He jabbed me again. I looked down and saw his arm was cut off at the elbow.

A wave took me back to Chester. He ordered two more pints of bitter. We shared a stool and watched the crowd. I was seeing double but I was happy. I felt very close to Chester, man to man; he knew what it was like to be living alone. His wife had run off with an interior decorator, leaving him with two kids.

I sometimes wished my wife would do the same. I could manage the kids.

Chester confided that he too had thought of training.

"It's an attractive idea, but I'm suspicious of it. I think I ought to become a doctor first, then a psychiatrist, and *then* an analyst. Sure, it's a long haul, but we're puers, we need to buckle down."

I peeled off with Melanie, a local gamin known to have a soft spot for colonials.

*

"That's all very well," scolded Rachel. "But what about Norman? You get loaded and stir the past, while he takes a back seat. Whose story is this, anyway?"

"Norman? Ah yes, I know him well," I said. "But I don't think about him unless he's sitting right in front of me."

Rachel laughed outright.

I sobered up.

"I'm not a machine," I said. "This is not a textbook, it's a process. One thing leads to another. It's like a snake weaving through the weeds. It'll get to where it's going, eventually, but meanwhile it savors the journey."

"Snake?" said Rachel. "Weeds?" She was genuinely puzzled. She needn't have been. I've used that image before.[5]

"Be patient," I said, "it's all germane."

---

[5] See *The Survival Papers*, p. 112.

I wasn't sure of that, but I trusted the process. I knew what I was doing, I just didn't know why I was doing it. To put it another way, as Arnold does, where you're headed and where you get to may be two different things.

*

My analyst heard me out. He was skeptical.

"You don't go into training because you can't think of anything else," he admonished.

By then I'd had a few sleepless nights. It seemed a crazy idea but I kept coming back to it.

"It's what I want to do," I insisted.

"Are you thinking of helping people?"

My messianic streak had come up more than once, especially in connection with my wife. We had spent several sessions on my inclination to save her from herself. A savior complex often goes hand in hand with a positive mother complex. It's another symptom of inflation. What you know, who you are, can save the world—starting with those closest.

"That hadn't occurred to me," I said, honestly.

I wrote to the Jung Institute in Zurich for information on training. It seemed like a pretty rigorous process and very expensive. I didn't see how I could manage it. I had the qualifications, but it would mean four or five years in Zurich, in continuous analysis, and students weren't allowed to work there. I was also told that many who started training did not finish.

"It is an uncertain endeavor which you would be wise to consider carefully," read the letter from the director of training. "The unconscious will have its say. One never knows where it will lead."

Four or five years! And nothing certain! Cripes!

I was as surprised as anyone when I found myself there a year later. So was Chester, who came soon after.

*

98 The Worm Turns

Norman came to the next session with a few books.

"Did you know," he said, "that in myths of the hero's night sea journey, the fish, usually a whale, figures prominently as a symbol of death and rebirth?"

I nodded.

"In Egyptian mythology," said Norman, "a fish is said to have swallowed the phallus of Osiris when it was chopped into fourteen pieces by his evil brother Set."

I nodded.

Norman looked at his list. "I read in the Book of Tobit that the gall of a fish restored the sight of Tobit, which is to say, psychologically, it made him more conscious."

I nodded. I'd missed that one.

"Listen to this," said Norman. He picked up a book by von Franz and read:

> Psychologically the fish is a distant, inaccessible content of the unconscious, a sum of potential energy loaded with possibilities but with a lack of clarity. It is a libido symbol for a relatively uncharacterized and unspecified amount of psychic energy, the direction and development of which are not yet outlined. The ambivalence regarding the fish derives from its being a content below the threshold of consciousness.[6]

Norman read a few more items from his notes, then sat back, quite pleased with himself.

"I've done my homework," he said.

"So you have," I nodded.

I appreciated this evidence that Norman was involved with his own process. I also had an impulse to pat him on the head

"It seems like I've tapped into the collective unconscious," said Norman, smugly.

I nodded. "No doubt, so does everyone else, every night."

That was not fair, said Rachel.

---

[6] *Introduction to the Psychological Interpretation of Fairy Tales* (Zurich: Spring Publications, 1973), p. 124.

I blushed. Norman didn't notice, he was looking into space.

"The real question," I said, "is what do fish have to do with you?"

Norman was thoughtful.

"I'm not sure, perhaps they're related to some potential of mine that wants to surface."

I wouldn't quarrel with that.

"Of course there's the shit," Norman smiled. "There's always more shit."

He became serious.

"Would you recommend me for training? I've got the application from Zurich. I've sent them transcripts of my degrees, but I need two references."

I always feel uncomfortable when it gets this far. I have nothing against anyone training to be an analyst. If that's where their energy wants to go, it's okay with me. Only I am reluctant to *recommend* them. I will confirm the hours we've had together. I will acknowledge their involvement with their own psychology. I will vouch for their moral fiber. Anything more, like saying whether they would make a good analyst or not, I balk at, because I never know. I don't even know what *is* a good analyst.

"Why do you want to go to Zurich?" I asked.

Norman looked directly at me.

"I've given it a lot of thought. I want to continue my analysis and I might as well be in training at the same time. Being an analyst is a tentative goal. I know it might not work out that way, I might not go the distance. But there's nothing else that attracts me."

Right on, said Rachel.

"It's expensive," I said, remembering the two-dollar coffees, the shocking grocery bills, the rent, the telephone bills, the fees for analysis, the constant search for black work and loans. God! Arnold almost didn't make it.

"I've saved some money. I've had my eye on a new computer," Norman said wistfully.

I thought of my lost Thunderbird. That kind of sacrifice is relatively easy.

"What about your family?"

Norman hesitated.

"Oh, they'll manage. Nancy's mother left her some money. It's never been touched."

"Have you told her?"

"As a matter of fact, I have."

Norman's eyes glistened.

Shit, said Arnold, get out the kleenex.

"And?" I said.

"Nancy dropped in on me a few nights ago. Quite cheery, she'd been shopping downtown. I listened to her natter on about her day, then I told her what I had in mind. She listened with tears in her eyes. I couldn't stand her pain so I gave it one last try. I said I'd like to get back together."

Norman didn't meet my eyes.

There, I said to Rachel, I told you so. She nodded. And there, she said, but for me, goes you.

"I offered Nancy the opportunity to come with me, with the kids. We'd go to Zurich as a family; we'd both be in analysis. There are English schools there. We'd have a chance to make a new life. As I talked it became quite an exciting idea."

Exciting, indeed. More like convenient. It would be easier than leaving Mother behind. It's scary out there on your own. Better the devil you know.

"An interesting possibility," I said.

Norman grimaced.

"It was a disaster. Nancy said the whole idea was an insult. She said she didn't need analysis and certainly didn't want it, especially after seeing what it did to me.

" 'I don't like you as you are,' she said. 'I hate what you've become. You're cold and distant. You used to be dependable, I don't know you any more.' "

Norman, dependable? said Rachel. Hush, I said, to each her own.

"Tears rolled down her cheeks," said Norman.

" 'What I need is someone to take care of me,' said Nancy.

"I was bewildered. I thought my proposal showed a willingness to do just that.

"It was not a comfortable evening. Nancy paced, squinting at my drawings. She said I could go to Timbuktu, but her responsibility was to create a stable home for the children.

" 'A man supports his family,' she said. 'You're deserting us.'

" 'You have money,' I countered. 'You're not dependent on me.'

"I thought of my earning potential as a practicing analyst. If money were the real issue, she was crazy not to encourage me to go to Zurich.

"I shook my head. 'Your attitude makes no sense to me.'

" 'You have no feeling,' said Nancy.

"She talked of her fears, crazy stuff—the chimney would collapse, terrorists would break in, a hurricane would knock down the house. How could she protect Ian and Jennifer from such calamities?"

Negative intuition, noted Rachel.

Yes, all those terrible possibilities. Anything that might go wrong, will. It's not only sensation types who feel like that. Intuition has a dark side too.

"What would they do without a father? she went on. If something happened to me, how would she keep their memory of me alive? What were my hopes and ambitions for them?

"This line of questioning mystified me. I have no ambitions for my children and I don't know how I'd like to be remembered. God! Is that up to me?

" 'I hope they grow up,' I said, at a loss.

" 'You haven't tried,' she said bitterly. 'You haven't given us a chance.'

"Well now, that really pissed me off, considering the past few years. I pointed out that I'd suffered too, now I'd had enough. I would like to have my family with me, I said, but if she wouldn't come I would make a life for myself.

" 'You're a selfish man,' said Nancy. 'You only think of yourself, you always have. You won't work on our relationship.' "

We had a hand in that, said Rachel.

So we did. I once told Norman that working on a relationship was a mug's game, not compatible with having one. To my mind, working on a relationship puts the cart before the horse. Work on yourself and a good relationship will follow. You can either accept who you are and find a relationship that fits, or twist yourself out of shape and get what you deserve.

"There was lots more," said Norman. "It went on like that for about four hours. My good intentions had turned to dust. Nancy cried almost the whole time. It tore me apart, but for once I was quite calm. Sure, I'm worried about her. She's in distress. What woman wouldn't be, on her own with two kids? But what can I do? I want to live. You know what? The stronger I feel, the less Nancy likes me."

"Hmm," I said.

"It got to be so late she stayed the night. We slept together in the one bed. She sobbed off and on. I tried to comfort her but she always pulled away."

"I woke up in the middle of the night with a dream: Nancy is distraught. She doesn't want us to separate. She holds out her arms. 'Don't you want to hug me?' she pleads. 'Yes, I do I do,' I answer, heartbroken, 'but it won't work.'

"And another: I'm on trial. It isn't clear what I've done. My lawyer is drunk, sleeping in a corner. I have no defense.

Norman shook his head. "I had an erection but I quelled it."

We sat in silence. My stomach was doing its number, having its say. It was hard to believe Norman still didn't understand what he was up against. Nor, indeed, how well he was handling it.

I thought of my analyst's comment after my wife and I had separated. Like Norman, I made some efforts at reconciliation. They were all ineffectual.

"Do not presume that anything you do for a woman can change her attitude toward you," he said.

This shocked me at the time—it was such a novel idea. I still find it hard to believe. Arnold doesn't, it's a rule of thumb with him. Don't expect anything from a woman, says Arnold, licking his numerous wounds, she'll whup your ass.

"Nancy is helpless and frightened, full of self-pity," said Norman. "She's a grown woman who needs her daddy. Why haven't I seen it before?"

I shrugged. It was hard to know where to start.

"Projection? Your own need for a strong mother?"

Norman looked miserable.

"I love her. Is there nothing I can do to help?"

The savior complex having its say. When would Norman realize that his wife was responsible for herself? Love? I thought not. It smacked more of need, desperation. Norman imagined that if his wife had some analysis she would respond to him. But it was just as likely she'd turn to someone else. Norman still didn't see his wife as she was. He still couldn't accept or reject her and live with the consequences. He still wanted her to be someone else.

This is how I put it to myself: There is no essential difference between Norman's wife and his mother complex. To fight the complex, he has to close his heart to her. Or you can look at it another way: if he gives in to his wife, he sacrifices his manhood; if he stands firm, he might grow up.

And Nancy? Well, it seemed to me she was whistling Dixie. Unless she could acknowledge that her attitude toward men interfered with her relationships with them—and with Norman in particular—nothing he said or did would have any effect. That's why she was offended when he suggested she go into analysis. The idea didn't come from her.

True, that's just an opinion. It isn't worth much without a knowledge of Nancy's dreams.

However, she was certainly feeling the effects of Norman's work on himself. The more independent he became, the less power she had over him. That's always a shock. When people get a handle on what drives them, they no longer relate to other people in the same old way. They're no longer tied to someone by a complex. They can choose. Relating to this new person takes some adjustment.

That was the motivation behind the formation of Alanon, the support group for friends and relatives of those who join Alcoholics

Anonymous. To continue a relationship with a reformed alcoholic, you have to change too. The same is true for the mates and friends of those in analysis.

All this went through my head while Norman sat on the edge of his seat, waiting for the Word.

"Is there nothing I can do?" he repeated.

I was tempted to speak my mind. But even if what I thought were true it was a realization that had to well up in Norman himself—like Pallas Athene, the winsome Greek goddess born fully grown from the head of Zeus. Now there's an anima with common sense, distanced from the Mother.

Otherwise, in days or years to come, he might blame me for the end of his marriage. I could take the heat, but it would be no favor to Norman.

"I don't know," I said, taking off my glasses.

Norman stopped at the door and turned to me. "Oh, what about Zurich?"

I hesitated, but I'd already decided.

"Yes," I said, "I'll give you a letter."

8
Invitation to a Beheading

"What a lot of needles there are, Malte, and how they lie about everywhere, and when you think how easily they might fall out. . . ." She tried to say this playfully, but terror shook her at the thought of all the insecurely fastened needles which might at any instant, anywhere, fall into something.
—Rainer Maria Rilke, *The Notebooks of Malte Laurids Brigge.*

"Now you've done it," said Rachel.

She had just finished the new chapter. It lay in her lap like a piece of chewed spaghetti.

"Done what?" I said innocently.

I was spraying the lawn with some stuff that's supposed to kill grubs. Every night an army of raccoons tore up the grass, looking for food. This had been going on for five years. I'd beat them yet.

"Finally it's clear," said Rachel. "Norman is going to Zurich. Norman is you, he must be!"

One summer I staked netting all over the grass. They dug up the stakes. The next year I put in plastic owls. The coons ate them.

"Not so fast," I said, "lots of people train as analysts."

"Not many who are so much like you."

"You'd be surprised."

She wouldn't, actually. Not much surprises Rachel.

"Anyway," I said. "He's not there yet."

"He's as close as dammit," said Rachel.

Put lights on, said the garden people, coons are night folk, coons don't like light. Well, yes, I thought so too until I sat by the pool and turned on the high beams. The coons rumbled in at midnight, big as bears, and scared me away.

"Close only counts in horseshoes," I answered.

I couldn't manage without Rachel. Still, she doesn't know everything. I have a say too.

"Besides," I said, "even if he gets there he might not finish."

"That's true," agreed Rachel. "He might make a better editor than an analyst."

She laughed. I thought it was a low blow.

"It's true, isn't it," insisted Rachel.

I shut off the sprayer and looked at her. I felt Arnold creeping over me. "What is truth? What is reality? There are only possibilities. I'm close to Norman, but he's his own man. He might have decided to go into real estate. I wouldn't stop him."

"You made him up," accused Rachel. "For goodness sakes, I even helped you!"

Yes, she did, but she didn't rewrite paragraphs twenty times until they felt right. It wasn't Rachel who at four o'clock in the morning was still at it, looking for the right word. It wasn't Rachel who conceived the structure, gave it form. She didn't dream about Norman, she didn't toss and turn in her sleep, wondering what he'd do next. And she didn't pay for the Scotch.

All the same, I was about to agree, just to keep the peace, when Arnold stepped in.

"Tell her the real truth," he said, "Norman made *you* up."

Gotcha!

Rachel bit her lip. She hadn't thought of that one. Nor, indeed, had I. She struggled with the idea and let it go.

"What about the choice between his life and Nancy's?"

"You heard him—he wants to live."

"Pooh," said Rachel. "Norman has no choice. That was your experience. You're making him turn out just like you."

Am I? I thought. A needle of doubt passed through my head. Have I created Norman in my own image? Was it a shared destiny from the beginning? Could he not have a life different from mine? Was all this just a self-indulgent scam? A perverse variation on Pygmalion? *My Fair Puer?*

Again Arnold rescued me.

Invitation to a Beheading 107

"Don't listen to her," he said. "Norman makes his own decisions. You only watch, a professional catalyst."

Now Rachel was annoyed.

"That's nonsense," she snapped. "Norman is your creation. He is what you make him."

Arnold was firm. "No," he said, "it's out of your hands."

I needed time to think, so I turned my back on both of them. They were still at it when I went to bed.

*

The next day I took out my notes and mulled them over. I thought about this creative process. Nobody knows what really goes on when you write a book. There are theories, but nobody *knows*. The only sure thing is that there are as many different ways to write as there are writers.

Some say they till the ground, plant the seed and watch it grow. For me it's more like assembling a patchwork quilt. My computer is little more than a sewing machine. I have the patches, it's the needles that give me a hard time.

I will tell you what Jung had to say on the subject. Of course he didn't *know* either, but he had some ideas. Jung was nothing if not eclectic. He wrote something on just about everything.

In volume 17 of the *Collected Works*, there are several essays that deal particularly with the creative way. One is on James Joyce, one is on Picasso; the two others are more general.

Here is Jung's basic standpoint:

> The practice of art is a psychological activity and, as such, can be approached from a psychological angle. Considered in this light, art, like any other human activity deriving from psychic motives, is a proper subject for psychology. This statement, however, involves a very definite limitation of the psychological viewpoint when we come to apply it in practice. Only that aspect of art which consists in the process of artistic creation can be a subject for psychological study, but not that which constitutes its essential nature. The ques-

tion of what art is in itself can never be answered by the psychologist, but must be approached from the side of aesthetics.[1]

"Huh!" said Rachel. "Already he's hedging."

She'd been hiding in the weeds, playing with the snakes I bet.

"No he's not," I said. "He's laying down ground rules. He's setting limits to what psychology can meaningfully say about art."

"Sure," nodded Rachel, "that's his way. He'll blather on for a hundred and fifty pages and at the end, in the very last paragraph, he'll admit he knows nothing at all."

I was surprised at Rachel's scorn. Perhaps she had not recovered from the tussle with Arnold. Usually she takes her licks and bounces right back. I thought about trading her in.

"I heard that," said Rachel. "Just like a man! You don't get what you want and your mind starts roving."

Cripes, if Rachel goes chauvinist I'll toss in the towel.

"Look," I said, "the way I understand it, Jung is saying that the process of creating is a legitimate area for psychological speculation. But psychology can't determine whether the end result is art or not. That depends on contemporary taste. Van Gogh, for instance, died poor. Today his work fetches millions. Kafka was not appreciated in his lifetime. Now his work is hailed as a milestone in the history of modern literature."

"So?" said Rachel. "It all comes down to we know what we like."

"Yah? Why do we like what we like?"

"Well," said Rachel, as if I were a dummling, "because it's art."

This would go nowhere.

"Okay," I agreed. "Never mind all the factors involved in what we like, the things we call art. But how did what we like, or not, come to be? Think about that. Why did Michelangelo sweat his guts out painting the Sistine Chapel on his back? Where did Leonardo da Vinci get the idea for flying machines four hundred years before they

---

[1] "On the Relation of Analytical Psychology to Poetry," *The Spirit in Man, Art, and Literature,* CW 17, par. 97.

existed? What inspired Jackson Pollock to throw paint at his canvas when nobody else did? What possessed Picasso?"

Rachel took that in. She was with me now, engaged. I gave her another example, closer to home.

"Where did the idea to write about Norman come from? Don't ask if he's real or not, or if it's art. How did I come to put all this energy into his story?"

"It wasn't my doing," said Rachel. She leered. "I'd just as soon fool around."

"Right! And it wasn't mine. I'd rather play pool any day, go for a swim or just dawdle. But here I am, glued to the computer, trying to write a book. So who's responsible?"

Rachel knit her brow. A wisp of hair fluttered on her cheek. She brushed it back. A good looking woman. I love her, I thought.

"God?" she offered.

Good grief! What does she have between her ears? Did she never hear of Nietzsche's famous line, "God is dead"? God used to be an okay explanation for *everything*. In this day and age, God is a minor player.

I shook my head. "I hardly think so."

And lucky too. If I did, I'd be out there with the rest of them, touting the Word. I'd have a program on prime-time teevee, turning lead into gold. I'd have a theme park dedicated to my mother. People who couldn't afford to would send me money. I'd put it in the bank and feel righteous. I'd be a goner.

"God, if he exists," I said, "has more important things to do. I hope."

Rachel inclined her head.

"Jung has an explanation," I said. "Listen to this":

The unborn work in the psyche of the artist is a force of nature that achieves its end either with tyrannical might or with the subtle cunning of nature herself, quite regardless of the personal fate of the man who is its vehicle. The creative urge lives and grows in him like a tree in the earth from which it draws its nourishment. We would do well, therefore, to think of the creative process as a living thing implanted in the human psyche.[2]

"God, nature, what's the difference?" said Rachel.
"Wait, I didn't finish."

In the language of analytical psychology this living thing is an *autonomous complex*. It is a split-off portion of the psyche, which leads a life of its own outside the hierarchy of consciousness. Depending on its energy charge, it may appear either as a mere disturbance of conscious activities or as a supraordinate authority which can harness the ego to its purpose.[3]

"Do you see? It's a *complex* that drives people to create."
Rachel found that hard to swallow.
"So artists are neurotic, is that it? Art is the result of neurosis?"
I shook my head.
"No, you misunderstand the nature of a complex. It's a feeling-toned idea that gets you by the throat. There's nothing intrinsically wrong with a complex, it's only neurotic when it gets in the way. You can be creative because of a complex, but what you produce still has to be shaped. You can't do that unless you have some distance from the complex. There are creative people who would do better work if they weren't so neurotic. And there are neurotics whose creativity is locked in the closet. Complexes are the key. Understand your complexes and it's a whole new ball game."

Rachel mused about that.
"Where do I fit in?"
"You're the bridge to what's going on down there. You mediate the contents of the unconscious. Without you I'd have nothing to work with. Thanks to you, it wells up in me. It's all there, I can see it. But it still has to be shaped. That's my job."

"I think I understand," said Rachel. "But what starts the creative process? What sparks the complex?"

---

[2] Ibid., par. 115.
[3] Ibid.

I leaned back. This is where it gets sticky. I could speak of archetypes, the collective unconscious. I could give examples from fairy tales, mythology and religion. I could cite literature from all over the world.

Yes, I could blather on for a hundred and fifty pages and come back to the same place.

"I don't know," I said. "It's a mystery to me."

Rachel folded her arms and smiled.

"That's what I said in the first place—*God.*"

*

In a lecture delivered in 1936, Jung states that from the psychological point of view there are five main groups of instinctive factors: hunger, sexuality, activity, reflection and creativity. He would have added religion as an instinct but he figured it was covered by reflection, the search for meaning.

The creative instinct, writes Jung, is, like the others, "compulsive, but it is not common, and it is not a fixed and invariably inherited organization":

> Its connections with sexuality are a much discussed problem and, furthermore, it has much in common with the drive to activity and the reflective instinct. But it can also suppress them, or make them serve it to the point of the self-destruction of the individual. Creation is as much destruction as construction.[4]

Hence those single-minded artists who neglect vast areas of life, including the other instincts: they hardly eat, think, make love or do anything else. They devote themselves entirely to their work. They create, but at what cost?

Franz Kafka fell into this category, and he knew it. Although he had to be alone in order to write, he realized that a preoccupation with himself diminished his life in other ways. He described his writing as

---

[4] "Psychological Factors in Human Behaviour," *The Structure and Dynamics of the Psyche,* CW 8, par. 245.

"an artificial, miserable substitute . . . for forebears, marriage and heirs."[5] That's the leitmotif that runs through his diaries. It's also any artist's dilemma, a constant conflict. How do you get the time, the energy, to find your voice, hone your tools, while living with other people?

Kafka is a good example of how a person can be overwhelmed by the creative urge, used by it. Which is to say, creativity may be instinctive but how you harness its energy is not. That depends on consciousness.

Great works of art are symbolic, pregnant with meaning. They have what my London friend Harry called echoing depths. According to Jung, that's because they come from the collective unconscious, a stratum of the mind that exists in everyone, a genetic heritage waiting to be activated.

At that level, the personal psychology of the artist plays a small part, or should. Writes Jung:

> Art receives tributaries from this sphere [the personal] too, but muddy ones; and their predominance, far from making a work of art a symbol, merely turns it into a symptom. We can leave this kind of art without injury and without regret to the purgative methods employed by Freud.[6]

"Purgative methods?" asked Rachel.

Jeez, does she never sleep?

"Freud thought that art, so-called, was the result of sublimating sexual conflicts," I said patiently. "Although he recognized that the end result of the creative process was to some extent independent of the person who created it, he felt that most artists, as individuals, were neurotic. Get them on the couch for a few years—four or five times a week—sort out their oedipal fixations, their sexual hang-ups, and Bob's your uncle. He realized they might lose their angels as well as their devils, but he thought they'd be a whole lot wiser and happier."

---

[5] *The Diaries of Franz Kafka,* 1914-1923, p. 207.
[6] "On the Relation of Analytical Psychology to Poetry," CW 17, par. 125.

"You mean art is a substitute for sex?" said Rachel.

I crossed my fingers.

"More or less."

Rachel looked skeptical.

"Listen, there's some truth in that," I said. "A lot of what's called art, written or visual, is just so much exhibitionism by neurotics. They never get past their personal psychology.

"Look at these drawings of Norman's. Are they art? I wouldn't say so. They're simply images of what was going on in him when he drew them."

"What do they mean?" asked Rachel. She moved around, looking at them from different angles.

"I don't know," I said. "They're thumbnail sketches of his personal psychology at a given point in time. It's his job to understand them, not mine."

"I kind of like them," said Rachel. "They have . . . well, a certain quality."

She smiled. "He might make a better artist than an analyst."

I was ready for that.

"Jung cautioned against confusing the creative process with what is properly called art. He did a lot of painting and sculpting when he was in trouble. He too was obliged to come to terms with the unconscious.[7] What he produced is quite astounding, but not substantially different from what anyone can come up with.

"Jung resisted an inner voice telling him that such things were art. Here's how he put it:

> What the anima said seemed to me full of a deep cunning. If I had taken these fantasies of the unconscious as art, they would have carried no more conviction than visual perceptions, as if I were watching a movie. I would have felt no moral obligation towards them. The anima might then have easily seduced me into believing that I was a misunderstood artist, and that my so-called artistic nature gave me the right to neglect reality. If I had followed her voice, she would

---

[7] See *C.G. Jung: Word and Image,* Bollingen Series XCVII:2, trans. Krishna Winston, ed. Aniela Jaffé (Princeton: Princeton University Press, 1979).

in all probability have said to me one day, "Do you imagine the nonsense you're engaged in is really art? Not a bit." Thus the insinuations of the anima, the mouthpiece of the unconscious, can utterly destroy a man.[8]

"That's clearly stated," I said. "Whatever comes out of you, whether written or painted or chiseled in stone, is a moral problem. That's true whether you call it art or not."

Rachel was frowning, caught in a complex of her own.

"Me, cunning?" she said.

I shrugged. "You have many faces."

"What if other people like what you create?" she said.

"So much the better. Then you can buy groceries too."

---

[8] *Memories, Dreams, Reflections,* trans. Richard and Clara Winston, ed. Aniela Jaffé (London: Fontana Library, 1967), pp. 211-212.

9

Rachel Pulls a Fast One

I have been deeply impressed with the fact that the new thing presented by fate seldom or never corresponds to conscious expectation.
—C.G. Jung, Commentary on
The Secret of the Golden Flower.

I handed Norman the letter I'd written. It was carefully worded. It wasn't a eulogy, but if you read between the lines you could tell I thought he was good material for training. It took me an hour to write it. I like to say what I mean without giving myself away. You can't do that in two minutes.

Norman read it and looked sheepish.

"Thank you," he said, looking out the window.

This wasn't like Norman. Well, not the one I knew.

"What's up?" I said.

He had trouble finding his tongue.

"The fact is," he said finally, "I've changed my mind."

"What?!" I could hardly believe it.

"I've been thinking," said Norman. "It's an elitist thing, this Jungian stuff, it's beginning to feel like a cult. Who can afford it but the very rich?"

I was speechless. I thought of the cab drivers, teachers, priests, social workers, students and others I'd worked with. They all made a real financial sacrifice for analysis. Of course I have a sliding scale, but none of them were wealthy. Norman himself wasn't. How could he say that? I felt torpedoed.

I stared at him.

"I've decided to go into real estate," said Norman.

I gasped, I couldn't help it.

Gotcha! said Rachel, killing herself.

You little minx, I said.

You raised the possibility, not me, she smiled.

So I did.

Or was it Arnold?

Somewhat chastened, I collected myself and started again.

10

The Lazarus Heart

"Lazarus Heart" was a vivid nightmare that I wrote down and then fashioned into a song. A learned friend of mine informs me that it is the archetypal dream of the fisher king. . . . Can't I do anything original?
            —Sting, Sleeve Notes on *Nothing Like the Sun.*

Norman arrived exuberant.

"It's all happening!"

He was barely able to contain himself. He thumped the table between us.

"I'm accepted!" he cried. "Zurich said yes!"

He handed me the letter. The C.G. Jung Institute would be pleased to receive him as a training candidate, beginning the next spring session. That was two months away. Time enough to arrange his life, settle his affairs.

Norman was beside himself with glee. He bowed to me. "I'm sure your letter helped."

He insisted I put some music on. I chose a Mozart flute concerto by the Swiss flautist Peter Lukas Graf.

"That's nice," said Norman, "but it's the wrong mood. Sting! Play Sting!"

My son had given me *Nothing Like the Sun* for Christmas. I put it on and we listened to the first track, "The Lazarus Heart":

> He looked beneath his shirt today
> There was a wound in his flesh so deep and wide
> From the wound a lovely flower grew
> From somewhere deep inside
> He turned around to face his mother
> To show her the wound in his breast that
>   burned like a brand

> But the sword that cut him open
> Was the sword in his mother's hand
>
> Every day another miracle
> Not even death could tear us apart
> To sacrifice a life for yours
> I'd be the blood of the Lazarus heart
> The blood of the Lazarus heart[1]

Norman was quiet now.

"It's the right mood but the words give me the shivers," he said.

I turned it off and looked at him.

"You're a lucky man," I said. "You know your wounds."

"It feels like a mixed blessing," said Norman.

"Give it time, Lazarus was resurrected."

Norman became earnest.

"Speaking of wounds, have you ever read Somerset Maugham's *Of Human Bondage?*" he asked.

"No," I lied, "tell me."

"I haven't either," said Norman, "but last night I saw the film. It's a classic, made in 1934 with Leslie Howard and Bette Davis. He plays a young doctor who falls in love with a street girl. She gets sick and he nurses her back to health. Then she toys with him— flirts with other men, keeps him at a distance and so on. He takes it all, one shit sandwich after another. He's so besotted he can't see what she is. It's all very sad and romantic—a devilish anima fascination. He has a club foot, a wound that will never heal. It reminded me of the fisher king in the Grail legend."

He looked out the window. "And of myself."

I nodded.

"I saw it with Nicole," said Norman. "Remember her? The one with the cape? I walked her home in a drizzle. She huddled close under my umbrella and said how much she enjoyed being with me."

Yes. The butterfly waltz and the mulingi shuffle.

---

[1] Music and lyrics by Sting, published by Magnetic Publishing Ltd., represented by Regatta Music/Illegal Songs Inc., administered by BMI.

"Nicole has a penthouse apartment near the university. It's just one big room. Not much furniture, abstract paintings on the walls, low lighting from a few discreet lamps. Everything's at floor level, Japanese style. She made us a pot of herb tea. I poked about in her records and put on Crosby, Stills and Nash. I lay on the water-bed listening to 'Lady of the Island' and watched her bustle around. I was happy.

"We drank our tea and smoked a joint, my own home-grown. We giggled a lot. God! Everything's funny when you're stoned. We bounced on the bed and pretended we were pirates.

"Nicole got into a flowered kimono and did some T'ai Chi. She's small and thin, very graceful. You'd never know she was over forty. She floated around the room like a hummingbird.

"Then she came to me. She stripped me naked and aroused me. That wasn't difficult, but she made it into a ceremony. When I was stiff as a board she got a couple of candles, about the same size as my dink, and set them up on saucers beside the bed. She lit the candles, turned the lights out and took off her gown. I was bemused but in no mood to object.

"She sat cross-legged on top of me and wove her fingers through my hair. 'Wicked,' she whispered, 'very wicked!' "

"Wicked?" I repeated.

"I think so," said Norman.

"Maybe it was Wicca," I suggested. "Wicca or wekken was a name for the ancient goddess religion, an esoteric cult active in northern Europe for hundreds of years. Some of the women burned as witches in the Middle Ages claimed to belong to it. Maybe it's been revived again. I know a bookstore in California called Feminist Wicca."

Norman shrugged. "Nicole is certainly no feminist. At least not the way I understand it. She's soft and pliant."

Pliant, eh? The word *wych* in Anglo-Saxon meant pliant. Nicole began to interest me.

"She chanted to herself while she fondled me," said Norman.

Casting a spell?

"She'd bring me right to the edge and then stop. Then she'd start again. The candles flickered, casting shadows. The music was low. 'Suite: Judy Blue Eyes' and 'Marrakesh Express' went right through me. I was in seventh heaven."

One of the classical attributes of witches was the magic wand, staff or rod. They were said to use it in conjuring up the devil. That's the origin of the modern divining rod for finding water. Was Nicole using Norman's member as a stand-in? Maybe that's what modern witches do, what with plastic broomsticks and all.

According to Funk & Wagnall's, you can spot a witch by some well-known tests. For instance, a witch can't weep, at most she sheds only three tears; she has a birthmark under her armpit or hidden elsewhere under her hair; she has long eyes; she has to stop when she sees a broom and count the straws—or count seeds, grains, holes in a sieve, letters on a written page, etc.

Long eyes? said Rachel, rolling hers.

Witches are no joke. They can fly and make themselves invisible. They assume different shapes at will. They have powers of divination and arcane knowledge of drugs. They can inhibit childbirth, cause illness or death and turn men into raving beasts.

Norman was smiling at the ceiling, still on the water-bed. No froth on his lips.

Comforting, but inconclusive.

"Tell me," I said, "Does Nicole have any birthmarks?"

"Not that I've noticed," said Norman. "She has two tattoos, though—a butterfly on one hip . . ."

Butterfly, an ancient image for *psyche,* the Greek word for soul.

". . . and a five-pointed star on the other."

A *pentagram!* During the Middle Ages such figures were scrawled on the doors of those suspected of witchcraft. The witch brigade saw the sign and torched the house.

"When I could stand no more, Nicole took her mount," said Norman. "She squared her shoulders and rode me. In the dim light she even looked like a jockey. She whipped me with a shoelace—honest!—and I responded. Plunging, dipping, a mighty rod of steel.

Twisting, turning, a fine fettle of flesh. Careful, steady, holding, pushing, rolling around . . .

" 'Heigh-ho! Heigh-ho!' she cried, slapping my sides, spurring me on.

"I was galloping now, down the home stretch, pounding the turf, clods whipping by, neck and neck, the winning post looming, we're at the wire . . .

" 'Now now!' cried Nicole, reveling, bursting through. 'Yes yes yes oh yes that's it you win you win,' and we were together, a photo-finish."

Norman wiped his brow.

Of course there are white witches too, they do nothing but good.

*

Norman survived Nicole, and so did I. One of the things about being an analyst is that you get to live vicariously. Every day is Peyton Place. You sit back and listen. You hear it all, the gamut of life, from juicy exploits to embarrassing disasters. You are there, you feel what it's like, but you never get involved. Your own life is not on the line.

You see people struggling with themselves and you agree with Rachel: There, you think, but for her go I.

It's a terrible trap. If you do that long enough, even Rachel gets fed up.

The great challenge for an analyst is to continue to live his own life. That means not being satisfied with crumbs from the tables of others. It includes doing just what he expects of those he works with: keeping a journal, giving serious attention to his dreams and emotional reactions.

In the analytic hour, an analyst has an artificial presence. A penumbra surrounds him, courtesy of the transference. He has a god-like aura, he seems invulnerable. The same is true of doctors, priests, teachers and therapists of any kind. It's a persona that goes with the territory. There's nothing wrong with it. It's useful as a protective screen and, as pointed out earlier, it may have a lot to do with whatever healing takes place.[2]

Outside the hour, however, an analyst is just like anyone else. He shops for food and does his laundry. He worries about his weight, his socks have holes, he snores. He has money problems, unruly children, conflicts that give him sleepless nights. He too has a garden that needs tending.

All this has nothing to do with his analytic persona. If he forgets that, he might as well be peeling potatoes.

"You've used that," said Rachel. "About writers, remember? Cyril Connolly said those not aiming at perfection might as well be peeling potatoes."

Cripes, there are needles everywhere.

Analysis is a *job*. It's interesting work, but it's still a job. It's true that people can be called to it—like Samuel in the Bible being called to serve God—but so can mechanics, chartered accountants, hairdressers and pimps be called to their work. The notion that being an analyst is more meaningful than being, say, a pimp, is merely a cultural bias.

Norman doesn't realize this yet. Although his reasons for wanting to train are valid, he is nevertheless to some extent seduced by the persona of the analyst, namely the confident, uncomplicated front I present to him. The nature of our relationship precludes my giving him more than a glimpse of who I really am and what my life is like. In his eyes I am someone special. I don't mind. Part of my job is to accept whatever projection he has on me. I know that at some point, if he continues to work on himself, he'll take it back. I know too that this may not happen until he himself sits in the other chair.

In the meantime, the way Norman sees me is a prominent factor in his motivation to become more conscious; it will get him through some difficult nights.

*

---

[2] See above, pp. 28-29.

In the following weeks Norman saw a lot of Nicole. Witch or waif, to my mind she was good for Norman. His guilt-free gambols with her paralleled his growing ability to distance himself from Nancy. Nicole was not a substitute for Norman's wife, as so often happens to men who split and find themselves a new woman but the same old frying pan; she was a different breed of cat.

In terms of his anima development, personified by Jung as Eve, Helen, Mary and Sophia,[3] Norman had left Eve and was high-flying with Helen.

Rachel popped up.

"Yes!" she said. "I remember the line from Marlowe, 'All is dross that is not Helen.' I love it!"

"So do I," I smiled. "But a little Helen goes a long way. You can't stick there forever either."

I went back to my notes.

The stages of the anima described by Jung are helpful, but only as a rule of thumb. In fact, men live psychologically in a harem. Any man may observe this for himself by paying attention to his dreams and fantasies. His soul-image appears in many different forms, just as a woman's femininity has myriad expressions.

In subhuman guise, the anima may manifest as snake, toad, cat or bird; on a slightly higher level, as nixie, pixie, mermaid. In human form, to mention only a few personifications modeled on the prominent goddesses in Greek mythology, the anima may appear as Hera, consort and queen; Demeter/Persephone, the mother/daughter team; Aphrodite, the lover; Pallas Athene, carrier of culture and protectress of heros; Artemis, the stand-offish, maidenly huntress; and Hecate, ruler in the netherworld of magic.

The assimilation of a particular anima-image results in its death, so to speak. That is to say, as one personification of the anima is consciously understood, it is supplanted by another. The previous anima-image is left behind, a precondition for the coming-into-existence of the next. Like the mythical phoenix, the new soul-image rises out

---

[3] See *The Survival Papers*, pp. 64-65.

of the ashes of the old; or, to use a different metaphor, the man's new wine—his spirit—needs new vessels.

Anima development in a man is thus a continuous process of death and rebirth. An overview of this kind is very important in surviving the transition stage between one anima-image and the next. Just as no real woman relishes being discarded for another, so no anima-figure willingly takes second place to her upstart rival.

In this area, as in so much else involved in a person's psychological development, the good is the enemy of the better. To have contact with your inner woman at all is a blessing; to be tied to one that holds you back is fatal.

While the old soul-mate clamors for the attention that now, in order for the man to move on, is due to and demanded by the new one, the man himself is up against it. The struggle is not just an inner, metaphorical one; it also involves his lived relationships with real women.

The resultant suffering and inner turmoil, the tension and sleepless nights, are comparable to what occurs in any conflict-and-decision situation. Inner disputes of this kind can only be resolved through what in religious terminology is called grace. In the language of analytical psychology it is seen as an intervention of the Self, the regulating center of the personality—the transcendent function, the unexpected, the *tertium non datur.*[4]

The anima-image that must be left behind is characterized in fairy tales as the false bride, while the new one is called the true bride. The essential difference between the two is captured in Marie-Louise von Franz's observation: "The truth of yesterday must be set aside for what is *now* the truth of one's psychic life."[5]

I have referred to the "faithless Eros" required for a man to leave his mother.[6] The same thing is necessary when an old and familiar soul-mate, one's inner guide in former times, has to be sacrificed.

---

[4] Ibid., p. 143
[5] *Redemption Motifs in Fairytales* (Toronto: Inner City, 1980), p. 85.
[6] *The Survival Papers,* p. 108.

Rachel reappeared, somewhat distraught.

"It sounds like you're getting ready to trash me," she said.

I hugged her. She cuddled up and listened.

Von Franz explains what Jung meant psychologically when he talked about the need for a faithless Eros:

> That would mean the capacity to turn away from time to time from a relationship . . . . The *puer aeternus*, in the negative sense of the word, very often tends to be too impressed, too weak, and too much of a "good boy" in his relationships, without a quick self-defense reaction where required.[7]

To "turn away" from a relationship doesn't necessarily mean to leave it. It may simply involve paying more attention to oneself than to the other person. But even this much is a heroic feat for a man with a positive mother complex. It requires a ruthlessness that is characteristic of his unsentimental shadow. If he is not up to it—which to someone he's involved with may look like a lack of relatedness, no heart—he will suffer the consequences: loss of soul. In spite of himself, the new anima-image has the energy; she will withhold it unless, and until, he gives in.

The seductive lure of the false bride manifests in real life not only as a tie to an unsuitable woman but also as the wrong choice in a conflict-and-decision situation. This is due to the regressive tendencies of the unconscious. Each new stage of development, each foothold on an increase in consciousness, must be wrested anew from the dragon-like grip of the past.

The work on oneself involved in doing this Jung calls *contra naturam*, against nature. That's because nature is essentially conservative. There is a lot to be said for the natural, primitive mind and the instincts that go with it, but not much in terms of consciousness.

"Whenever a process has reached a culmination as regards either its clarity or the wealth of inferences that can be drawn from it," writes Jung, "a regression is likely to ensue."[8]

---

[7] *Puer Aeternus*, p. 47.
[8] *Psychology and Alchemy*, CW 12, par. 239.

The individual experiences this as listlessness, an unaccountable loss of energy, or, at the other extreme, as an inflated sense of self-worth.

Inflation is involved here because a man who has won a relationship to his anima, at whatever level, already feels himself to be king of the castle. He could leap mountains, kill seven giants at a blow. And he doesn't need any kind of dope to feel that way.

The great danger in assimilating previously unconscious psychic contents is that you become proud and overconfident, dangerously liable to overextend yourself. The inflated ego believes the war has been won, when only a local battle has been fought. Jung describes it like this:

> Paradoxically enough, inflation is a regression of consciousness into unconsciousness. This always happens when consciousness takes too many unconscious contents upon itself and loses the faculty of discrimination, the *sine qua non* of all consciousness.[9]

Jung was referring here to the collective hubris in Western societies that led to the First World War, but the same thing can be seen in the individual: war with oneself, inner strife between the old, false bride and the new, true one; a breakdown in functioning due to being maladapted to the changed circumstances of one's inner world; in short, another—or perhaps the first—midlife crisis.

If the individual does not wake up at this point, even worse may result. The further you go in the process of self-discovery, the further there is to fall. As Jung puts it:

> If the demand for self-knowledge is willed by fate and is refused, this negative attitude may end in real death. The demand would not have come to this person had he still been able to strike out on some promising by-path. But he is caught in a blind alley from which only self-knowledge can extricate him. If he refuses this then no other way is open to him. Usually he is not conscious of his situation, either, and the more unconscious he is, the more he is at the mercy of unforeseen dangers: he cannot get out of the way of a car

---

[9] Ibid., par. 563.

quickly enough, in climbing a mountain he misses his foothold somewhere, out skiing he thinks he can just negotiate a tricky slope, and in an illness he suddenly loses the courage to live. The unconscious has a thousand ways of snuffing out a meaningless existence with surprising swiftness.[10]

"That's scary," said Rachel.

"It is," I agreed, "but read the newspaper. It happens every day."

The appearance of a new stage of the anima, then, whether it wells up within or presents itself as a fascination for a real woman, may be seen as a call to a new level of consciousness. That's the true bride. Whether you embrace it/her or not—actually or symbolically—you have to take the attraction seriously.

Not becoming conscious when you have the possibility of doing so was always accounted by Jung to be the worst sin, for if you don't live up to an inner possibility it turns negative.

Rachel was intrigued.

"I can see there's a difference between what you call a false and a true bride," she said, "but how do you tell one from the other?"

"It's not easy," I said. "They don't come labeled. A lot depends on a man's age, his position in life and how much work he's done on himself—particularly the extent to which he's already differentiated his soul-image from the other complexes teeming in his psyche.

"Theoretically, there are two basic types of false bride. One is an anima figure—or an actual woman—who leads a man into the fantasy realm, away from timely responsibilities in the outside world. The other is an inner voice—or again a real woman—that would tie a man to his persona when his real task is to turn inward, find out what's behind the face he shows others.

"The first type is commonly associated with the idealistic attitudes of a younger man. You see this in the disinclination to compromise, a rigid response to the reality of everyday life."

"Revolutionaries and anarchists," nodded Rachel, "they would change the world."

---

[10] *Mysterium Coniunctionis,* CW 14, par. 675.

"Right," I said. "In any society there is a need for change, but only those who pay their dues have a hope of making it happen. The rest are pissing in the wind."

Rachel crinkled her nose. She's not all that fond of colloquial expressions.

"The second type of false bride is normally involved with the regressive tendency of the unconscious in later life, when, for the health of the psyche, material values should take second place. Regression is evident in those who make feverish efforts to reclaim their youth—much younger companions, a compulsion about fitness, hair transplants and so on.

"There's no hard and fast rule, however. An older man with too much unlived life may have to descend into the whore's cellar, so to speak, as part of his individuation process. The younger man with no ideals may be forced to develop some. One must beware, too, of rationalizations that are simply wish-fulfillments of the ego."

Rachel took that in and asked: "How does all that affect a man's relationships with women?"

"It's no different from any psychological content," I said. "The bride of either type, when not recognized as an inner reality, appears in the outside world through projection. If a man's anima is lonely and desperate for attention, he will fall in love with dependent women who demand all his time and energy. The man with a mother-bound anima will get tied up with women who want to take care of him. The man not living up to his potential will fall for women who goad him on.

"The bottom line is that whatever qualities a man doesn't recognize in himself—call them shadow, anima, whatever—will confront him in real life. Outer reflects inner, that's the general rule. If there are any psychological rules that are valid always and everywhere, that's one of them."

Rachel frowned.

"The way you put it, women are left with a dog's breakfast."

"That's up to them," I said. "They have a choice too. Von Franz says there is no distinction between an unconscious woman and a man's anima.[11] The implication is that an unconscious woman can be coerced into being whatever a man wants. But it's just as true the other way around. Unconscious men are easily seduced by a woman's animus. In relationships there are no innocent victims."

Rachel registered shock.

"Read all about it in Esther Harding's *The Way of All Women*.[12] She put it better than I can. The more differentiated a woman is in her own femininity, the more able she is to reject whatever unsuitable role is projected onto her by a man. This forces the man back on himself. If he has the capacity for self-examination and insight, he may discover in himself the basis for false expectations. Failing inner resources on either side, there is only rancor and animosity."

I reflected.

"A lot of situations like that end in separation or divorce. That's disruptive but psychologically not so bad. Many unions limp along in morbid soil to the advantage of no one, least of all the children involved. The tragedy is that the opportunity for self-realization is unrecognized or refused, and then repeated."

Now Rachel's head was swimming. I could see it in her eyes. Normally languid pools, they had become fathomless.

"Let's go back to the false and true brides," she said. "Is what you want a reliable guide?"

"No. Wants are all ego. Over and against what you want is what the unconscious thrusts upon you for the overall good of the psyche. That's the true bride. It usually appears as something new and unexpected. It's an aspect of the Self, the archetype of wholeness, which Jung describes as 'some scarcely definable arbiter, . . . a centre of balance.'[13]

"This becomes clearer as you pay attention to yourself. Remember the Grail legend, where the fisher king's wound can only be healed if

---

[11] *Archetypal Patterns in Fairy Tales* (Lectures at the C.G. Jung Institute, Zurich, 1949-50, transcribed by David Hart), p. 78.
[12] New York: Harper Colophon, 1975, chapter 1, "All Things to All Men."
[13] *Two Essays on Analytical Psychology*, CW 7, par. 311.

the hero asks the right question? When Parsifal is first confronted with the phenomenon of the Holy Grail, he is overcome with awe and reverence. He doesn't ask what it has to do with him. The Grail vanishes and he has to wander many years through the forest—the unconscious—before he comes upon it again, asks the question and heals the fisher king.

"Understanding your own psychology, like recognizing the true bride, is a matter of asking the right questions, again and again. Do that long enough and the Self is activated. Von Franz says that having a relationship with the Self is like being in touch with an 'instinct of truth.' There is an immediate awareness of what is right and true for the personality, a truth without reflection:

> One reacts rightly without knowing why, it flows through one and one does the right thing. One says Yes, or No, sometimes doing one thing and sometimes the other, and can carry on without intermission . . . . That is the action of the Self becoming immediate, and only the Self can accomplish this. On a higher level, it is the same thing as being completely natural and instinctive, when one can discern between the false and the true. . . . With the help of the instinct of truth, life goes on as a meaningful flow, as a manifestation of the Self.[14]

"In practical terms, it comes down to a man *knowing* what is right for him. 'He has a strong feeling of what should be and what could be,' writes Jung. 'To depart from this divination means error, aberration, illness.'[15]

"That's why Norman is off to Zurich and not staying with his family," I pointed out. "Events in his outer life reflect what's taken place inside. It's not exactly what he wants, but he knows what he needs."

"It seems so ruthless," said Rachel.

"Yes it does. But Norman is following his inner truth, his true bride. Like when I left Canada to be a struggling writer. I wouldn't

---

[14] *Alchemy: An Introduction to the Symbolism and the Psychology* (Toronto: Inner City Books, 1980), pp. 172, 174.
[15] *Two Essays,* CW 7, par. 311.

—or couldn't—have done that without being nudged by my shadow. Norman is in a similar boat. Once you know what you need, you really have no choice."

Rachel was having trouble keeping her eyes open. She'd had enough, and so had I.

"Thus endeth the lesson," I said.

I made a back-up copy and shut the computer down. I stared out the window.

Light was breaking in the east. A taxi passed. A garbage truck rumbled through. The paper-boy dropped his bundle and moved on.

A glowing sun heaved up, a great semicircle of fire, clearing the decks for a new day. It would be steaming hot, again. I made another note to look into air-conditioning.

I thought of the scarab beetle. It pushes a ball of dirt in front of it. As the sacred Khepri, it was worshiped in ancient Egypt as the embodiment of the rising sun and of the supreme creator god Atum. Khepri symbolized the self-regenerating life force. In Heliopolis it was seen as the god of transformation and symbol of the birth of the new sun from the womb of Mother Earth.

A vagrant kicked a can. The lady next door padded to the curb in her dressing gown, calling her cat. Two joggers waved at me without breaking stride.

I yawned.

A passage of Kafka's came to mind. I've used it before, but it's one of my favorites.

> Whoever leads a solitary life, and yet now and then wants to attach himself somewhere; whoever, according to changes in the time of day, the weather, the state of his business and the like, suddenly wishes to see any arm at all to which he might cling—he will not be able to manage for long without a window looking on to the street.[16]

---

[16] "The Street Window," in *The Penal Colony* (New York: Schocken Books, 1961), p. 39. See also my *Personality Types*, p. 97.

Rachel raised her head.
"Yes," she said. "We all need somebody."

11

The Beginning of the End

The unconscious is useless without the human mind. It always seeks its collective purposes and never your individual destiny. Your destiny is the result of the collaboration between the conscious and the unconscious.
—C.G. Jung, *Letters.*

I said good-bye to Norman with mixed feelings. He arrived in a jaunty mood, wearing a gaudy red tie and a blue blazer.

It was our anniversary. Two years ago he turned up crying in my office. My secretary gave him tea and he spilled it on his pants.

"I celebrated last night," he said. "I went to the opera. I saw *La Bohème* for the first time. God, it was all there!"

"It was?" I asked.

"It's about a sick anima," said Norman. "I've always been a sucker for the frail beauties. Puccini takes it to the extreme." He gestured vaguely. "I see what I was into."

Norman now had a legal separation from Nancy. Psychologically he was in pretty good shape; which is to say, he knew what he had to work on. He was still seeing Nicole but he wasn't thinking of marriage.

"We have something special, but I'm happy living on my own," he said airily, as if it were nothing. "She loves me and can show it. And I can feel it." He grinned from ear to ear. "I'm a simple country boy. That's all I ever wanted."

I smiled. "You've come a long way Charlie Brown."

I did not begrudge my appreciation now because Norman had earned it. In the past year we'd been through almost as much as the first. He survived the break with his wife because he took his plight seriously and he worked on himself. You can't ask for more than that. Well, I don't.

Norman was formless when I first saw him—a puddle of water, a bowl of jelly. Now he had some substance. You could see it in his body—the way he held his head, the way he walked, the way his hands moved. And in his eyes.

There was an air of quiet dignity about him. He accepted himself. I respected that.

"I saw a new version of Pinocchio on television," said Norman. "Remember where he goes to Gepetto, the old craftsman who made him out of a block of wood? 'I want to go to school,' says Pinocchio. 'I want to be a real boy.'

"In the original Gepetto gives him his blessing. 'Good for you, that's a noble ambition,' he says, something like that.

"Well in this modern version Gepetto looks down his nose at Pinocchio and says, 'Stay wood! There are lots of real boys. Stay wood and act real. We can join a circus and make a fortune!'"

We laughed.

"That would make it a variation on Peter Pan," said Norman.

I nodded.

In fact I saw it rather differently—Gepetto as a wise old man counseling his creation not to lose the dynamic energy that goes with youth. Norman was going to Zurich. That's Pinocchio wanting to be real. I had nothing against that. Norman had a pressing need to grow up—to incorporate some senex values. But if he threw out the puer he'd be no better off.

I didn't say this to Norman. I trusted that if he went too far in one direction, his own psyche would demand a balance.

Norman had brought a dream with him.

"A woman approaches me with a child. It's a boy, a year old, maybe a bit more. The woman is vaguely familiar. She asks me for religious instruction. I tell her she's made a mistake, I'm not a priest. She smiles and hands me the child. I woke up quite mystified."

"What do you make of it?" I asked.

"I suppose the woman is an aspect of my anima, one I don't know very well."

I nodded. "And the child is new life, new possibilities."

"Hey," said Norman,""it's just over a year ago that I left Nancy. That would have been the birth of something new, wouldn't it—the child?"

I agreed. "It would put the conception back in the early months of analysis."

Such dreams are not uncommon. The unconscious is surprising. It often seems to be outside of time and space as we know it. But at times it throws up images that fit in quite well with the sequence of events in everyday life. That is the reality of the psyche.

"What about the religious angle," I said.

Norman shrugged. "You know me, I don't go to church."

I went to my bookshelf and took out volume 11 of Jung's *Collected Works*. I leafed through it as I spoke. "Jung believed that a neurosis in later life is never cured without the development of a religious attitude."

"I'm an atheist," said Norman firmly.

"Are you?"

I found the passage I wanted. "Listen to this: 'The term "religion" designates the attitude peculiar to a consciousness which has been changed by experience of the *numinosum*.' "[1]

I flipped pages. "And here Jung says that a man in a conflict situation has to rely on 'divine comfort and mediation . . . . an autonomous psychic happening, a hush that follows the storm, a reconciling light in the darkness . . . secretly bringing order into the chaos of his soul.' "[2]

Norman became pensive.

"That's very interesting," he said finally, "I never thought of it that way."

At the door we embraced. I'd grown attached to Norman.

---

[1] "Psychology and Religion," *Psychology and Religion,* CW 11, par. 9.
[2] "A Psychological Approach to the Dogma of the Trinity," ibid., par. 260.

"Look after the child," I said. "Write if you get work."

To myself I added: *And stay wood.*

We shook hands and I helped him on with his coat. Spring had come, but it was still a bit chilly. The snow hadn't completely melted, but here and there some buds had surfaced. Yesterday Arnold told me it was time to spray the plants.

"Tell me," I said, "did I influence you?" I blushed.

Norman halted in his tracks. He turned to me, astonished. "Of course. My direction was clear but how I got here was not. I would still be nothing without you."

I demurred.

"And have I made a difference to you?" said Norman.

"Yes," I admitted. "At times I was breathless."

Norman beamed. "No kidding."

*

It was my last appointment for the day. In the past two years I had cut my practice to the bone. Now I often had whole days to myself, completely free. In the winter I played squash. On hot summer days I lay beside the pool, watching the elephant-clouds.

I wandered down to the basement and browsed through the stacks, looking at the pictures. It was very satisfying. I thought about the difference Norman had made to me.

Well, I wasn't bored any more.

Epilogue

"I expected something quite different," said Rachel.

She had just finished the last chapter.

"Different?" I said defensively.

"It's almost the same as the last chapter of *The Survival Papers,*" said Rachel.

"It couldn't be radically different. I was just filling in the blanks."

Rachel took that well.

"Okay," she acknowledged, "what's next?"

I assumed an enigmatic air.

"Even as we speak," I said, "offers are pouring in from Hollywood."

That wasn't quite true. My sister-in-law's cousin had sent a copy to a friend of his who knew a woman in Sausalito whose boyfriend was a writer who had connections with a film producer in Beverly Hills. Still, as Arnold pointed out, there were possibilities.

"There are rumors that Rob Redford is crazy to play Norman and Madonna is bidding for the part of Nancy. I don't say they're true, but I can't gainsay them."

Rachel raised her eyebrows.

"Go on," she said.

"Rod Steiger and Jack Nicholson have both expressed interest in Arnold, and Jessica Lang is desperate to play Nicole. John Candy wants Walt. Red Buttons would be a natural for Chester. A few small parts, like Monique, the vicar, Harry and the boys and so on, are still up for grabs."

I sat back and polished my nails.

"There's talk of a nation-wide search to find a good baby Ian."

"That leaves the analyst and me," said Rachel.

"I liked Judd Hirsh as a shrink in *Ordinary People*. Intelligent, very cool, laid back. There's no rush, I'll keep the options open."

"And me?" smiled Rachel. "Who would play me?"

I fidgeted.
"Come, speak up!" said Rachel. Just like the Red Queen.
"Are you ready for this?"
"I'm waiting."
"Cher."

Some of the characters depicted in this book don't exist.
The author is indebted to those who do.

Index

abaissement du niveau mental, 35
abandonment, 66, 70, 101
absent father, 65-66
Addiction to Perfection, 66n
alchemy, 24, 34, 40
Alcoholics Anonymous, 103-104
ambivalence, 20-21
analytic process, 22-30, 43, 62, 89-90, 121-130, 135
analytic training, 88-90, 93-97, 99-100, 104, 117, 130
anima, 11, 16, 19, 40, 92, 104, 113-114, 118, 123-131, 133, 135
animus, 66, 87, 129
Arnold, 12-13, 18, 21-22, 34-39, 45-46, 57, 59, 63-64, 66, 74, 77, 91, 94, 97, 99-100, 102, 106-108, 116, 136
art, 107-114
Asclepius, 27
astrology, 34, 59, 92
Athene, 104, 124

Baba-Yaga, 87
Beatrice, 67-69
bees, 67-69
Bertine, Eleanor, 31
boredom, 33-35
Boris, 16, 66
bride, false and true, 124-130
brothers, 32-35
butterfly, 120

Cain and Abel, 32
Carnegie, Dale, 47, 54
cats, 60-61, 123
cause and effect, 69-70

Chee Chee, Benjamin, 61
Chester, 94-97
child, 92, 134-136
Christ, 21, 92
collective unconscious, 98, 111-112
complex(es) (*see also* mother, father, savior), 25-26, 67, 87, 103, 110-111, 114, 127
conflict, 16-17, 20-21, 88, 122, 124-125, 135
Connolly, Cyril, 52, 122
consciousness, 17, 25-30, 35, 72, 112, 125-130
contra naturam, 125
countertransference, 27
creative process, 107-114
cross-cousin marriage, 27-28

depression, 23, 29, 34
dream(s): 24, 27, 43, 82, 103, 135
  of brother, 32
  of child, 134-135
  of department store, 40
  of Eleanor, 16
  of fish, 91
  healing, 27
  of peeing, 39-40
  of police, 40
  of shit, 91
  of woman with whip, 40

ego, 26, 32, 43, 128
elephants, 60, 70, 92
empathy, 29, 66
Enkidu, 33, 39
Eros, 58, 124-125
expectations, *see* projection

140 Index

fairy tales, 87, 92, 124-125
faithless Eros, 124-125
false bride, 124-130
father complex, 65-66
feeling function, 35
felix culpa, 17
Finches, 55-56, 95
fish, 91-92, 98-99
fisher king, 92, 117-118, 129-130
frame, of analysis, 62
Freud, Freudian, 27, 32, 62, 69, 94, 112
Fromm, Erich, 42

Gilgamesh Epic, 33, 39
Gladys, 44-46, 51
God, 109-111
grace, 124
Grail legend, 92, 118, 129-130
guilt, 82-84

Harding, Esther, 129
Harry and the boys, 52-56
healer, inner, *see* wounded healer
hero, 66, 87, 92, 98, 125, 130
Hillman, James, 29
Horus and Set, 32

idealism, 127-128
identification, 29, 85
incubation, 27
individuation, 24, 128
inflation, 29, 33-34, 90-91, 97, 126
instinct(s), 26, 111, 125, 130
instinct of truth, 130
intuition, 34-36, 95, 101
island, 26, 30
Jung, C.G., 15, 23, 26, 34-36, 53, 62, 68, 70, 85, 88, 90, 93, 107-113, 115, 123, 125-127, 133, 135

Kafka, Franz, 40, 108, 111-112, 131
Khepri, 131
Kierkegaard, 53
knot, in stomach, 28, 58, 64, 83, 102
Kusmitch, Nikolai, 25

La Bohème, 133
Lawrence, D.H., 60
Lazarus, 118
"Lazarus Heart, The," 117-118

Martin, P.W., 72
Maugham, Somerset, 118
meaning, 31, 44-50, 127, 130
Monique, 75-77
mother complex, 12, 16, 37-38, 40-41, 64, 66, 83-87, 97, 100, 103, 117-118, 125

Nancy, 13, 16, 40, 58-72, 77-87, 100-103, 123, 133, 135
nature, 37-38
neurosis, 110, 112, 135
nicknames, 81
Nicole, 89, 118-121, 123, 133
Nothing Like the Sun, 17

Of Human Bondage, 118
opposites, 16, 34, 36-38, 66, 68, 92
Osiris, 98

peeing, 39-40
pentagram, 120
persona, 17-18, 26, 67, 86, 121-122, 127
Peter Pan, 134
Pinocchio, 134
police, 40
possibilities, 12, 31, 35-40, 86, 92-94, 100-101, 106, 116, 127, 137

Pregnant Virgin, The, 66n
prima materia, 24, 92
projection, 22, 26-29, 41, 64, 81, 103, 122, 128-129
psyche, 120
Psychology and Religion, 135
"Psychology of the Transference," 23
puella, 66
puer, 40, 66, 77, 91, 96, 106, 125, 134

Rachel, 11-13, 20, 23, 26, 32, 40, 42-43, 45, 54, 56, 59, 63-67, 77, 81, 84-87, 90, 96, 98-101, 105-116, 120-132, 137-138
regression, 34, 82, 125-126
relationship(s), 67-68, 101-102, 125, 128-129
religion, 134-135
Rigoletto, 74
Rilke, Rainer Maria, 25, 105
Roger, 50-51

savior complex, 88, 97, 103
scarab, 131
science, 69
"Sea-Hare, The," 92
Self, 92, 124, 129-130
senex, 56, 134
sensation function, 34-36
sentimentality, 82
sex, sexuality, 40, 75-77, 84, 111, 113, 119-121
shadow, 28, 32, 34-37, 92, 128, 131
shit, 15, 91, 99
sibling rivalry, 32
siren, 40
snake(s), 27, 33, 39, 96, 108
soul, 27, 62, 92, 120, 123-125, 135

St. George, 64
Sting, 117-118
suggestion, 93
suicide, 23, 29
Survival Papers, The, 11-12
symbiosis, 68
synchronicity, 68-70, 89, 94

Talmud, 92
tertium non datur, 124
thinking, 69
time, 25
Tobit, Book of, 98
transcendent function, 124
transference, 22-29, 42, 88, 121
true bride, 124-130
typology, 34-39, 67-68

unconscious: 17, 23, 26-29, 97, 114
 and anima, 129
Unquiet Grave, The, 52
urine, 40

"Virgin Czar, The," 87
visions, 24
von Franz, Marie-Louise, 35, 98, 124-125, 128-130

Walt, 45-48, 50-52, 56-57
Way of All Women, The, 129
Wendy, 55-56
Wicca, 119
witch(es), 42, 61, 83, 87, 119-121, 123
Woodman, Marion, 66n
wounded healer, 23, 27-29, 118

yang-yin, 92
Ygor, 61, 95

Studies in Jungian Psychology by Jungian Analysts

Limited Edition Paperbacks

Prices and payment in U.S. dollars (except for Canadian orders)

1. The Secret Raven: Conflict and Transformation.
Daryl Sharp (Toronto). ISBN 0-919123-00-7. 128 pp. $13
A practical study of *puer* psychology, including dream interpretation and material on midlife crisis, the provisional life, the mother complex, anima and shadow. Illustrated.

2. The Psychological Meaning of Redemption Motifs in Fairytales.
Marie-Louise von Franz (Zurich). ISBN 0-919123-01-5. 128 pp. $13
Unique approach to understanding typical dream motifs (bathing, clothes, animals, etc.).

3. On Divination and Synchronicity: The Psychology of Meaningful Chance.
Marie-Louise von Franz (Zurich). ISBN 0-919123-02-3. 128 pp. $13
Penetrating study of irrational methods of divining fate (I Ching, astrology, palmistry, Tarot cards, etc.), contrasting Western ideas with those of so-called primitives. Illustrated.

4. The Owl Was a Baker's Daughter: Obesity, Anorexia and the Repressed Feminine. Marion Woodman (Toronto). ISBN 0-919123-03-1. 144 pp. $14
A modern classic, with particular attention to the body as mirror of the psyche in weight disturbances and eating disorders. Based on case studies, dreams and mythology. Illus.

5. Alchemy: An Introduction to the Symbolism and the Psychology.
Marie-Louise von Franz (Zurich). ISBN 0-919123-04-X. 288 pp. $18
Detailed guide to what the alchemists were really looking for: emotional wholeness. Invaluable for interpreting images and motifs in modern dreams and drawings. **84 illustrations.**

6. Descent to the Goddess: A Way of Initiation for Women.
Sylvia Brinton Perera (New York). ISBN 0-919123-05-8. 112 pp. $12
A timely and provocative study of the need for an inner, female authority in a masculine-oriented society. Rich in insights from mythology and the author's analytic practice.

7. The Psyche as Sacrament: C.G. Jung and Paul Tillich.
John P. Dourley (Ottawa). ISBN 0-919123-06-6. 128 pp. $13
Comparative study from a dual perspective (author is Catholic priest and Jungian analyst), exploring the psychological meaning of religion, God, Christ, the spirit, the Trinity, etc.

8. Border Crossings: Carlos Castaneda's Path of Knowledge.
Donald Lee Williams (Boulder). ISBN 0-919123-07-4. 160 pp. $14
The first thorough psychological examination of the Don Juan novels, bringing Castaneda's spiritual journey down to earth. Special attention to the psychology of the feminine.

9. Narcissism and Character Transformation. The Psychology of Narcissistic Character Disorders. ISBN 0-919123-08-2. 192 pp. $15
Nathan Schwartz-Salant (New York).
A comprehensive study of narcissistic character disorders, drawing upon a variety of analytic points of view (Jung, Freud, Kohut, Klein, etc.). Theory and clinical material. Illus.

10. Rape and Ritual: A Psychological Study.
Bradley A. Te Paske (Minneapolis). ISBN 0-919123-09-0. 160 pp. $14
Incisive combination of theory, clinical material and mythology. Illustrated.

11. Alcoholism and Women: The Background and the Psychology.
Jan Bauer (Montreal). ISBN 0-919123-10-4. 144 pp. $14
Sociology, case material, dream analysis and archetypal patterns from mythology.

12. Addiction to Perfection: The Still Unravished Bride.
Marion Woodman (Toronto). ISBN 0-919123-11-2. 208 pp. $15
A powerful and authoritative look at the psychology of modern women. Examines dreams, mythology, food rituals, body imagery, sexuality and creativity. A continuing best-seller since its original publication in 1982. Illustrated.

13. Jungian Dream Interpretation: A Handbook of Theory and Practice.
James A. Hall, M.D. (Dallas). ISBN 0-919123-12-0. 128 pp. $13
A practical guide, including common dream motifs and many clinical examples.

14. The Creation of Consciousness: Jung's Myth for Modern Man.
Edward F. Edinger, M.D. (Los Angeles). ISBN 0-919123-13-9. 128 pp. $13
Insightful study of the meaning and purpose of human life. Illustrated.

15. The Analytic Encounter: Transference and Human Relationship.
Mario Jacoby (Zurich). ISBN 0-919123-14-7. 128 pp. $13
Sensitive exploration of the difference between relationships based on projection and I-Thou relationships characterized by mutual respect and psychological objectivity.

16. Change of Life: Psychological Study of Dreams and the Menopause.
Ann Mankowitz (Santa Fe). ISBN 0-919123-15-5. 128 pp. $13
A moving account of an older woman's Jungian analysis, dramatically revealing the later years as a time of rebirth, a unique opportunity for psychological development.

17. The Illness That We Are: A Jungian Critique of Christianity.
John P. Dourley (Ottawa). ISBN 0-919123-16-3. 128 pp. $13
Radical study by Catholic priest and analyst, exploring Jung's qualified appreciation of Christian symbols and ritual, while questioning the masculine ideals of Christianity.

18. Hags and Heroes: A Feminist Approach to Jungian Therapy with Couples.
Polly Young-Eisendrath (Philadelphia). ISBN 0-919123-17-1. 192 pp. $15
Highly original integration of feminist views with the concepts of Jung and Harry Stack Sullivan. Detailed strategies and techniques, emphasis on feminine authority.

19. Cultural Attitudes in Psychological Perspective.
Joseph Henderson , M.D. (San Francisco). ISBN 0-919123-18-X. 128 pp. $13
Shows how a psychological attitude can give depth to one's world view. Illustrated.

20. The Vertical Labyrinth: Individuation in Jungian Psychology.
Aldo Carotenuto (Rome). ISBN 0-919123-19-8. 144 pp. $14
A guided journey through the world of dreams and psychic reality, illustrating the process of individual psychological development.

21. The Pregnant Virgin: A Process of Psychological Transformation.
Marion Woodman (Toronto). ISBN 0-919123-20-1. 208 pp. $16
A celebration of the feminine, in both men and women. Explores the wisdom of the body, eating disorders, relationships, dreams, addictions, etc. Illustrated.

22. Encounter with the Self: William Blake's *Illustrations of the Book of Job*.
Edward F. Edinger, M.D. (Los Angeles). ISBN 0-919123-21-X. 80 pp. $10
Penetrating commentary on the Biblical Job story as a numinous, archetypal event.
Complete with Blake's original 22 engravings.

23. The Scapegoat Complex: Toward a Mythology of Shadow and Guilt.
Sylvia Brinton Perera (New York). ISBN 0-919123-22-8. 128 pp. $13
A hard-hitting study of victim psychology in modern men and women, based on case material, mythology and archetypal patterns.

24. The Bible and the Psyche: Individuation Symbolism in the Old Testament.
Edward F. Edinger (Los Angeles). ISBN 0-919123-23-6. 176 pp. $15
A major new work relating significant Biblical events to the psychological movement toward wholeness that takes place in individuals.

25. The Spiral Way: A Woman's Healing Journey.
Aldo Carotenuto (Rome). ISBN 0-919123-24-4. 144 pp. $14
Detailed case history of a fifty-year-old woman's Jungian analysis, with particular attention to her dreams and the rediscovery of her enthusiasm for life.

26. The Jungian Experience: Analysis and Individuation.
James A. Hall, M.D. (Dallas). ISBN 0-919123-25-2. 176 pp. $15
Comprehensive study of the theory and clinical application of Jungian thought, including Jung's model, the structure of analysis, where to find an analyst, training centers, etc.

27. Phallos: Sacred Image of the Masculine.
Eugene Monick (Scranton/New York). ISBN 0-919123-26-0. 144 pp. $14
Uncovers the essence of masculinity (as opposed to the patriarchy) through close examination of the physical, mythological and psychological aspects of phallos. **30 illustrations.**

28. The Christian Archetype: A Jungian Commentary on the Life of Christ.
Edward F. Edinger, M.D. (Los Angeles). ISBN 0-919123-27-9. 144 pp. $14
Psychological view of images and events central to the Christian myth, showing their symbolic meaning in terms of personal individuation. **31 illustrations.**

29. Love, Celibacy and the Inner Marriage.
John P. Dourley (Ottawa). ISBN 0-919123-28-7. 128 pp. $13
Shows that without a deeply compassionate relationship to the inner anima/animus, we cannot relate to our intimates or to God, to the full depth of our ability to love.

30. Touching: Body Therapy and Depth Psychology.
Deldon Anne McNeely (Lynchburg, VA). ISBN 0-919123-29-5. 128 pp. $13
Illustrates how these two disciplines, both concerned with restoring life to an ailing human psyche, may be integrated in theory and practice. Focus on the healing power of touch.

31. Personality Types: Jung's Model of Typology.
Daryl Sharp (Toronto). ISBN 0-919123-30-9. 128 pp. $13
Detailed explanation of Jung's model (basis for the widely-used Myers-Briggs Type Indicator), showing its implications for individual development and for relationships. Illus.

32. The Sacred Prostitute: Eternal Aspect of the Feminine.
Nancy Qualls-Corbett (Birmingham). ISBN 0-919123-31-7. 176 pp. $15
Shows how our vitality and capacity for joy depend on rediscovering the ancient connection between spirituality and passionate love. Illustrated. **(Foreword by Marion Woodman.)**

33. When the Spirits Come Back.
Janet O. Dallett (Seal Harbor, WA). ISBN 0-919123-32-5. 160 pp. $14
An analyst examines herself, her profession and the limitations of prevailing attitudes toward mental disturbance. Interweaving her own story with descriptions of those who come to her for help, she details her rediscovery of the integrity of the healing process.

34. The Mother: Archetypal Image in Fairy Tales.
Sibylle Birkhäuser-Oeri (Zurich). ISBN 0-919123-33-3. 176 pp. $15
Compares processes in the unconscious with common images and motifs in folk-lore. Illustrates how positive and negative mother complexes affect us all, with examples from many well-known fairy tales and daily life. **(Edited by Marie-Louise von Franz.)**

35. The Survival Papers: Anatomy of a Midlife Crisis.
Daryl Sharp (Toronto). ISBN 0-919123-34-1. 160 pp. $15
Jung's major concepts—persona, shadow, anima and animus, complexes, projection, typology, active imagination, individuation, etc.—are powerfully presented in the immediate context of an analysand's process. And the analyst's. We are there as they both struggle with the conflict between the security of a hard-won, successful lifestyle and an inner imperative that demands a total reassessment of self—with no guarantees. Illustrated.

36. The Cassandra Complex: Living with Disbelief.
Laurie Layton Schapira (New York). ISBN 0-919123-35-X. 160 pp. $15
A close look at how hysteria manifests in the female psyche, and why it threatens patriarchal values. Includes clinical material and an examination of the role of powerfully intuitive, medial women through history. Shows how unconscious, prophetic sensibilities can be transformed from a burden into a valuable source of conscious understanding. Illustrated.

Prices and payment (check or money order) in U.S. dollars

Please add $1 per book (bookpost) or $3 per book (airmail)

INNER CITY BOOKS
Box 1271, Station Q, Toronto, Canada
M4T 2P4